Many may dream of one day wearing Navy Wings of Gold, but few truly appreciate what is required to earn those Wings and move from the street to the Fleet. In this book, "Bio" shows how he climbed from college student to experienced naval flight officer. Aircraft have changed, but that process continues on. Here's a great read for any aviation enthusiast, and especially for anyone considering a career in Naval Aviation.

—Vice Admiral "Streak" Chanik, USN (Ret.),
former F-14 pilot and Topgun instructor

I couldn't put Dave Baranek's book down—he put me right in the cockpit of his aircraft and made me feel like I was a Navy RIO running intercepts on bad guys. Dave wanted to be a pilot; so did I, but our eyesight wasn't quite good enough, so we both chose to become backseaters. It doesn't matter where you sit in a fighter or bomber or reconnaissance plane—it's all about flying; military flying; taking planes to the edge of the envelope. It's about tough training and besting the bad guys if and when you meet up with them. BEFORE TOPGUN DAYS In Dave takes you from the day he reports to NAS Pensacola as an utter novice until he straps on an F-14 Tomcat and flies with a carrier at sea. What I liked best about the book is being part of his demanding training—day by day, event by event. I love the book. This is an aviator's book – for anyone who loves to reach for the sky.

—Wolfgang W. Samuel, Colonel, USAF (Ret.),
author of GERMAN BOY and IN DEFENSE OF FREEDOM

Baranek describes a relatively little-known area of Navy flight training, that of the F-14 radar intercept officer or RIO, the guy-in-the-back, as skilled as his pilot up front but not as familiar to the average reader of modern aviation literature. Only someone who has actually experienced the demanding instruction required to earn this unique position in a flight crew, followed by the months of deployments in the Fleet in a combat-ready F-14 squadron, could hope to tell this story in such deeply personal detail. As one who tried but failed, I found myself filling in many of the blanks as I read this lively adventure story. Great job, Bio!

—Peter Mersky, author of WHITEY, F-8 vs. MiG-17, and U.S. MARINE CORPS AVIATION SINCE 1912

# BEFORE
# TOPGUN DAYS

# BEFORE TOPGUN DAYS

## The Making of a Jet Fighter Instructor

**DAVE "BIO" BARANEK**

Skyhorse Publishing

Skyhorse Publishing books may be purchased in bulk at special discounts for sales promotion, corporate gifts, fund-raising, or educational purposes. Special editions can also be created to specifications. For details, contact the Special Sales Department, Skyhorse Publishing, 307 West 36th Street, 11th Floor, New York, NY 10018 or info@skyhorsepublishing.com.

Skyhorse® and Skyhorse Publishing® are registered trademarks of Skyhorse Publishing, Inc.®, a Delaware corporation.

Visit our website at www.skyhorsepublishing.com.

10 9 8 7 6 5 4 3

Library of Congress Cataloging-in-Publication Data is available on file.

Cover design by Rain Saukas
Cover photo credit: Dave Baranek

Print ISBN: 978-1-63450-655-7
Ebook ISBN: 978-1-63450-656-4

Printed in China

To my wife, Laura.

# CONTENTS

# Introduction

In my book *Topgun Days*, I took you with me into the high-speed, high-stakes arena of Navy jet fighters: day and night carrier operations, dogfighting in the F-14 Tomcat, and teaching the best of the best as a Topgun instructor. We ejected from a doomed fighter jet, faced a Topgun murder board, and flew "MiG-28s" for the movie cameras. We put it all on the line and did it all.

No, not all. There was a prelude, a time that had its own excitement, dangers, and humor. That was Navy fighter training in the 1980s. It started in Pensacola, where they took college boys and taught us how to slug it out in aerial combat and come back alive. Then they sent us on to San Diego to fly the mighty F-14 Tomcat and learn about the real-world flying we would soon be doing.

It's time to begin. Time to turn back the calendar to a time before Topgun days.

ONE

# An Ensign Begins

Like many teenagers, I had a dream. I wanted to fly jet fighters. To me, that dream was as tangible as the shiny jets I saw at airshows. In my youthful imagination, flying jet fighters would be the ultimate in adventure; zooming through the sky without limits, in control of a powerful machine, meeting any challenge that might arise. I could never imagine the many steps along the path to reaching that dream, I only knew that others had done it, and I would do whatever it took to do it too. I was going to fly fighters.

After a decade of dreaming—no, *seeing* myself flying those jets—I took the first real step toward reaching my goal. Three weeks after graduation from college, I was in Pensacola, Florida, to start flight training.

You can hardly talk about flying in the Navy without mentioning Pensacola. In 1914 the Navy set up its first flying school in this busy little city. To this day, one thing every Navy flier has in common is the aviation indoctrination course at Naval Air Station (NAS) Pensacola.

Some officers come to Pensacola from the US Naval Academy in Annapolis, some from the Reserve Officer Training Corps program—well-known as ROTC, with units at dozens of colleges across the country—and some begin their Navy training in Aviation Officer Candidate School, where they receive intense military indoctrination after earning their college degrees. Each program has its pluses and minuses.

ROTC worked for me, and I attended Georgia Tech in Atlanta. The Navy ROTC program included taking classes called Naval Science and going on four-week "summer cruises" that exposed us to what life would be like after we graduated. We got a glimpse of the various career choices: submarines, surface ships, aviation, or joining the Marine Corps (which had its own career fields). This helped some students to figure out what they wanted. For me, it confirmed that I was on the right path. I'd known since grade school that I wanted to fly fighters. I had devoured everything I could find about military aircraft, and I even drew airplane pictures while sitting in class, all through high school and college.

Like most who dream of flying, I yearned to be a pilot. But then, during my freshman year of college, my eyesight began to deteriorate. I knew that to be a fighter pilot you had to have 20/20 vision. Eyesight doesn't go bad overnight, so for several months I talked to many people about it, including a few fortunate souls whose vision had actually improved over time. But by the time I got glasses, my vision was 20/40. There was no kidding myself. I was not going to be a fighter pilot.

I had considered Air Force ROTC but fortunately chose Navy instead, because the Navy was introducing a spectacular new fighter, the F-14 Tomcat. This was good news! The F-14 had a two-person crew, and the second crewman didn't need 20/20 vision. I could wear glasses and fly fighters! I wouldn't be a pilot, but I would be in a fighter. My dream was alive.

During our senior year of college, my ROTC classmates and I filled out "dream sheets" requesting the kind of duty we wanted to go into after graduation. What an appropriate name for these requests, in my case. Our instructor told us we had to write something in every block. So I did: aviation as my first choice, surface ships as second choice, and something else as third. This was the first of many "doors," instances where my future was uncertain. I knew where I wanted to go, but would have to be selected or meet qualification requirements.

We were repeatedly reminded that the most important factor in our assignments was "needs of the Navy," a phrase we would hear repeatedly throughout our careers. During the months of waiting for the decision, I occasionally imagined myself on a sleek destroyer, slicing through gray seas in the open ocean. I decided that if that's where the Navy sent me I would make the best of it. But it didn't come to that. I was ecstatic to learn, about three months before graduation, that I had been selected for aviation training. There would be many more doors ahead. As each of these decision points approached I did what I could to give myself the best chance, but sometimes I just had to trust my fate and the wisdom of those making the decision.

At graduation for the Class of 1979, I was commissioned an ensign. By July I was sitting in a crowded Navy classroom in Pensacola with thirty-eight other freshly minted officers, mostly young men, but at least one young woman as I recall. With painted cinder block walls and fluorescent lights, the room was crammed full of displays and charts that served their purposes but looked like antiques that belonged in a museum. My new friends and I were not there to judge, for this was the start of our new lives. We had competed for these seats and won them over many others. We would be here for six weeks of classroom, physical fitness, survival, and other training. I couldn't wait to get started.

Our teachers were Navy lieutenants and Marine Corps captains, many of them a mere five years older than we were. They wore the same uniform we did, and only a handful of years before had sat in the same classroom. Now they carried not only technical knowledge and instructor skills, but a credibility and confidence gained from a few years in "the Fleet." They had presence. They had attitude. They were what we wanted to be.

Most of us were Navy ensigns, joined by a few Marine Corps second lieutenants and Coast Guard ensigns. A typical day in class felt a lot like college: we started at 7:00 or 8:00 a.m. and finished in the afternoon. But unlike some college classes, everything we were studying would directly apply to our profession for the next few years, such as basic aerodynamics and aircraft engine fundamentals. Classroom sessions were peppered with lessons from accident investigations, and all of the instructors added their own tales of mishaps or great saves. These were called "war stories," whether they happened in combat or not. At this point in my training, stories about flying still seemed distant, still my dream.

It was too early to be very competitive; most of us just wanted to get a sense of the new environment and our friends. We got to know each other around the slide-show training programs in the library (state of the art in 1979), practicing on the low-intensity obstacle course near the officers' quarters, hanging out at various night spots in Pensacola, and washing the cars we had recently bought when we started getting paychecks.

These first cars were commonly known as "ensign-mobiles." Most were fairly modest, which was a small disappointment to me. I expected a parking lot full of sports cars and convertibles. Instead, I found a Mercury Capri, a five-year-old Plymouth Valiant sedan, and other sensible cars. One guy had a Nissan 280-Z, another had a Firebird with a serious high-performance engine. I had a seven-year-old Mustang convertible, model year 1972. I don't recall any Corvettes or Porsches.

To keep life simple, I chose to live on the base in the bachelor officers quarters, which we all called the BOQ. From the street it looked like a mid-range hotel, with several buildings of two or three stories. Each student had the equivalent of a studio apartment, with a shared living room and kitchen. After four years of living in dorms at college it was comfortable enough for me.

In decades past, living on the base had been common for military officers and enlisted personnel. For those assigned to ships, many lived on the ship. Policies that required personnel to be in uniform when entering or leaving the base, and while on the base, made it simpler and more convenient to just live there. But as society evolved and US military forces became all-volunteer (the draft ended in 1973), such policies were relaxed and personnel started to move off-base. Only about one quarter or less of my Pensacola classmates lived in apartments, but percentages increased as time went on.

It became obvious that my fellow flight students in aviation indoctrination—known as AI—ran the full spectrum of interest and knowledge. Some didn't know a Tomcat from a Hawkeye. Others were firmly committed to what they wanted to fly, whether it was a P-3 Orion maritime patrol aircraft, A-6 Intruder medium bomber, helicopter, or another in the variety of Navy aircraft. Our majors in college were varied, too. Many of us were engineers, but some majored in business, agronomy, geology, animal science, or psychology (me). Some had been high school football stars; others were certifiable geeks. Several had already held "real jobs" before becoming officers, such as grocery store manager or construction worker. A few were married and had started families. Most of us were twenty-one to twenty-four years old, though a few were almost thirty.

We had at least one female officer in our class. She wasn't "the first"—the first women pilots in the Navy earned their wings in 1974, and this was five years later—but women aviators were still rare in the military.

One of the subtle pleasures of this time was our exposure to Naval Aviation lingo, the verbal shorthand that allows "Those Who Know" to communicate efficiently, and also separates them a little more from everyone else. Most terms were related to an aircraft or a mission, but some referred to people. Future pilots were known as Student Naval Aviators—SNAs. Many people think of "aviator" as a generic term for anyone who has something to do with operating an airplane, but when the letters are capitalized—Naval Aviator—it means a *pilot,* the person who operates the throttles, stick, and rudder.

The designation of non-pilots is more complex. In the Navy, officers who fly but are not pilots are called Naval Flight Officers, or NFOs. As students we were SNFOs. The NFOs who went to fighters were called RIOs, for radar intercept officer. It's pronounced "rio," as in Rio Grande. Those who went to A-6s were bombardier-navigators, BNs. NFOs who flew in other aircraft were known by various other terms according to their crew responsibilities. Assignment to specific aircraft types was still in our futures, so for a time we were all SNFOs. There was no catchy way to say this, so we were usually just called students, or "studs," which was how we saw ourselves.

For convenience, I will use aviator with a lower-case "a" for both pilots and NFOs.

I was an SNFO. Sure, I had dreamed of being a pilot, but by the time I got to Pensacola I was happy with my new goal: RIO, the back-seater in the new F-14 Tomcat fighter. Some friends who faced the same choice decided they didn't want to fly if they couldn't be *pilots*, so they decided, early on, not to join the military, or they opted for the shipboard Navy. Not me. I'd rather fly than float.

On that very first day, we were issued our personal flying gear. Because it would be months before we actually flew, this was possibly intended to keep us excited through the challenges ahead, until we got real job satisfaction. At the scheduled time, we all drove over to "Flight Gear Issue," a small cinder block warehouse on the far side of the base, where we received:

- boots, safety
- gloves, flying

– helmet, flying
– knife, survival

These and many other accessories were identified by the military "noun, adjective" convention. Each item was recorded in our logbooks.

Of all the items, one of the most important to us was the flight suit. It was made of flame-resistant Nomex fabric and looked like the coverall of any comfortable garage mechanic who likes loose-fitting olive green. Flight suits were commonly called "bags." We wore bags all day long when we could, but sometimes at the squadron we had to contend with orders to be in a standard uniform when not flying. Bags were great for the Officers' Club, where they helped the aviators stand out from ship-drivers, submariners, and all others. More mature officers knew that everyone contributed to mission accomplishment, but in the early days this distinction was priceless.

I think most guys wore something like gym shorts and T-shirts under their bags. Later we would be comfortable enough in bags to skip the gym shorts. I suspect there were some adventurous guys who just . . . liked the feel of Nomex, shall we say.

One other item issued that day actually surpassed the flight suit in desirability. It was recorded as *jacket, flying*—the brown leather aviator's jacket recognizable worldwide. This jacket by itself was reason enough for many of us to sign up. It just looked cool and had become a cultural icon. Some of the farsighted among us left theirs unblemished, but I joined the group that had a few patches sewn on my new jacket. Like bad tattoos, I regretted them several weeks later, but it was too late. There were stitch marks in the leather.

We all survived day one. We were quite excited to get back to our rooms or apartments that afternoon with all of this gear. It brought us a tangible step closer to our futures, even though there were still many trials before our first flights. Back in my room I dressed up in everything and looked in the mirror. The gear fit me, but I knew I had a long way to go before I fit the gear.

My class spent day two at the Naval Aerospace Medical Institute (NAMI) receiving thorough physical exams to verify our eligibility for flight status. Those who were found deficient were washed out of the program; as we put it, they got the "NAMI whammy." We'd all had physicals just before graduation from college or the Academy, so most of us had no surprises.

The eye doctors at NAMI Pensacola, however, were a special group. They determined the career path of many a young hopeful by ruling whether he really had 20/20 vision and could continue into SNA training, or didn't and thus would become an SNFO. For some, this decision came down to a final session in the exam chair. There were stories of memorized eye charts, sleeping for twelve hours before the exam, and various other techniques by which a fence sitter could squeeze into pilot training. For me the eye test was a non-event: I wasn't even close to 20/20 and I was truly happy to imagine myself as a Tomcat RIO.

Our third day started at the swimming pool. The Navy was big on swimming, which seems obvious, but it was a problem for several students in every class, including mine. We didn't simply swim. We swam various strokes. We treaded water until the instructor became bored. We jumped off platforms, then swam underwater while wearing boots and the baggy flight suit. Various aquatic qualifications would be part of every Navy flier's entire career.

I was amazed to see some of my contemporaries trembling with fear before they jumped from the platform fifteen feet above the water. We weren't asked to perform demanding dives, only survival-related techniques. Once we entered the water, we had to swim twenty to thirty feet underwater, break the surface and splash water away from our faces, then swim another short distance underwater. This was to simulate getting away from an aircraft crash by swimming underwater in case there was burning fuel on the surface, and then clearing a spot to grab a breath. Most of the class had no problem, but we could see the fear in a few—who then displayed the guts to jump in and conquer it. In my class, everybody qualified.

After swimming, we made timed runs on an obstacle course. Our obstacle course included walls we had to leap onto and climb over, large timbers to hurdle, overhead bars that required swinging from one rung to the next, and a few others. We had to hustle to get through, but it wasn't exhausting: three minutes, fifty-one seconds was the maximum time allowed. I made it in 3:23.

The next week we again mixed classroom sessions with physical fitness tests. In the afternoon we were timed on a "confidence course" (similar to an obstacle course but less challenging), a 1.6-mile run, and a one-mile swim. I thought the standards were reasonable; I had never been a serious athlete, but I managed respectable showings in all events, including some basic boxing classes.

If you've ever tried parasailing, you were probably towed aloft by a boat driving along the beach of a glitzy resort. We, however, were towed behind a gray Navy pickup truck in an open field, with not a bikini in sight. But one ride gave us a benign exposure to a parachute landing, should we ever have to return to earth *sans* flying machine.

Over the next few weeks of AI we completed some more qualifications in aviation physiology. One of the more peculiar tests was an electroencephalogram (EEG) administered with your eyes closed and a bright strobe light flashing in your face. Our instructor explained that a small percentage of us would have an adverse experience and be disqualified from flying helicopters. To this day I don't know whether he was serious. When the strobe flashed we saw vivid spiral patterns—with our eyes closed. It was amusing and intriguing; the patterns were as vivid as if you were looking at them wide-eyed with wonder. The nurse ended my test before I had seen enough. None of us had an adverse reaction.

We were introduced to the dangers of high-altitude flight in the low-pressure chamber, or "altitude chamber." This is a large box that looks like a walk-in freezer, big enough for more than a dozen students on bench seats. We listened over headsets as an attendant in the chamber narrated events. He was on oxygen, we were not. Air was pumped out of the chamber, simulating the thinning atmosphere at high altitudes—the altitudes that we would soon traverse. Thinner air means less oxygen, with detrimental effects known as hypoxia beginning shortly after climbing through 10,000 feet.

One memorable visual aid was a partially inflated surgical glove that hung limp overhead, but gradually expanded into a five-finger balloon as pressure in the chamber was reduced. Sure enough, we all experienced hypoxia as the simulation took us to around 20,000 feet. Each of us was given tasks to perform, such as signing our names or playing patty-cake with the person next to us. It was silly, but under the effects of hypoxia this child's play soon became impossible. Point made, the attendant instructed us to use the oxygen masks by our seats, and we quickly returned to full cognizance. The experience imprinted on us the importance of wearing oxygen masks at high altitudes.

We also took our turns riding the dynamic ejection seat. For this we proudly wore our virgin flight suits, which transformed us into young men and women trying to be serious while feeling like six-year-olds at the county fair. The seat shot required us to strap into a mockup of an aircraft seat that was mounted in a simple gray box, with sturdy rails rising out of it and angled back about 15 degrees from vertical. The track went up about twenty feet.

Here you go. You assume the proper body position for ejection—head up, back straight, elbows tucked in. Now you yank hard on the yellow-and-black striped handle between your legs. This triggers a compressed air charge that blasts the seat—and you—up the rail. For a split second, you feel like you weigh four or five times your normal weight; in aviator jargon, that's pulling 4 or 5 g. It's over quickly, but the ride and the lecture that follows make a big impression on you. It sure did on us.

We also continued our aviation-related academic endeavors, to be sure. But these experiences introduced us to the physical sensations and some of the dangers of flying. During these sessions I felt like I was on an extreme vacation. In the back of my mind I knew that the government doesn't send people on extreme vacations, that later there would be a payback in sacrifices and risk taking. But the careful preparations made the risks seem manageable, and the sacrifices worthwhile.

TWO

# Dunkers and Draggers

Demands on our performance steadily increased as the hardware got more complex. The Monday of our fourth week, after classroom exams on navigation, engines, and aerodynamics, after boxing and the psychedelic EEG, after the pressure chamber and dynamic seat shot, we faced a device that was at once humorous and intimidating: the Dilbert Dunker. It was invented during World War II to teach fliers how to escape from a plane that crashes into the sea and flips over, and its original name had stuck.

Mounted at the edge of a big, beautiful swimming pool, the Dilbert Dunker was a crude aircraft cockpit: outer shell, seat, stick, and windscreen. It had no canopy, but it had seatbelts. The cockpit was mounted on a pair of rails that angled down about eight feet and continued into ten feet of water. For a thrill seeker with a short attention span, it was perfect.

Like every Navy flight student since the 1940s, I strapped in. The instructor quickly reviewed the procedures he had explained to the group just minutes before, and then the Dilbert Dunker rolled down the rails and plunged into the pool. It made a big splash, and I took a quick gulp of air as it submerged with me still strapped inside. At the end of its track the cockpit flipped upside down, in slow motion due to the drag of moving in water. The water cascading into my now-inverted nose was an unwelcome distraction.

After the contraption stopped moving I oriented myself as instructed, undid my buckles and straps, and pushed free. Being inverted, I headed first toward the bottom of the pool, then arched up toward the surface. There were several Navy scuba divers watching, so I knew it would be difficult to drown. But for students just four weeks into our Navy careers, the anticipation, the sound of the Dunker trundling down its short track and splashing into the pool, and the instructions to remember underwater were intimidating. In the end, we focused on the task assigned, and our class didn't lose anyone.

Having gained a dose of confidence, we proceeded the next day to an even more diabolical device, the Helo Dunker.

At some time in their careers, many Navy people would find themselves in a helicopter over water, flying to or from a ship. The Navy analyzed mishaps and determined that most helicopter crashes were survivable, but some passengers had drowned because they could not get out of the cabin after water impact. So the Navy developed the Helo Dunker. Looking like a giant green barrel, the Helo Dunker tested up to eight students at a time. It was lowered into a deep pool and rotated when underwater. We had to wait until all movement stopped before unstrapping from our seats and finding our way out. We did this four times to qualify, the last two with blindfolds to simulate a nighttime crash.

As I strapped into a seat for the fourth run, my clothes were wet from the previous runs. I lowered my blindfold. The device descended into the pool. I heard the splash and felt the water at my feet rising. The barrel quickly submerged and water rose to my waist, then suddenly to my neck. Now the water felt cold. I tried to take that last full breath at the optimum instant, knowing that if I messed up I would have thirty or forty seconds to think and act before I could return to air. Once we were submerged, the device rotated purposefully but in a random direction—this time it rotated through the inverted, stopping 210 degrees from upright.

I waited for all motion to stop, since divers were watching to make sure we followed instructions. I placed both hands at my waist and released my seat belt. The fact that we were inverted was incidental in this underwater escape scenario, save for the now familiar sensation of water up my nose. Others in the drum had already unstrapped and started for the single window designated as an exit for this run. That was good, they were probably feeling the pressure in their lungs, but I was still comfortable. I moved out of my seat and grabbed the seat in front of me as a guide to the . . . hey, tennis shoe in the face!

It didn't really hurt, and I didn't have the option to complain, so I stayed focused on the escape. I worked hand over hand as I followed a path to the exit, keeping track of those feet ahead with my hand, not my face. They seemed to be headed for the correct window. I grabbed the window frame, pulled free, and just floated for a moment to make sure I knew which way was up. Then I swam to the surface, felt real air on my face, and took off the blackout goggles. I was done!

Most of my fellow passengers were nearby, bursting to the surface with the exhilaration of real crash survivors. One guy came up on the other side of the pool and the observing divers told him the bad news: he'd used the wrong exit window and had to go again to qualify. But overall it was another good day, with no permanent damage and more stories to tell at the bar. It impressed on us the importance of paying attention to instructions and remaining calm in unusual situations.

The Navy found a marked reduction in fatalities after they began Helo Dunker training. That's a good return on investment. In the bigger picture, attention to detail and realistic training were common themes, important additions to skill and passion if we wanted to do well in the potentially dangerous careers we were launching into.

The pool wasn't finished with us. We also had to learn to untangle ourselves from a parachute that had draped over our heads after we splashed into the water. I had grown up swimming in pools and at the beach, so I felt very comfortable in the water and enjoyed these trials. Any student who kept calm and followed procedures could meet the requirements with little difficulty. And it sure beat "Marco Polo" for spending time in a swimming pool.

The last two weeks of water survival training shifted from pools to the open water of Pensacola Bay. The water was calm, but it was a big step mentally from the controlled environment of the swimming pool, where you could see the bottom. The new situations built on our previous lessons.

Late one morning we gathered at an ancient seaplane hangar by the bay. Wooden piers jutting into the bay held winches and cables with hooks on them. Nearby we saw racks of old parachute harnesses. Like the plot of a slasher movie, we would have figured out what was coming even if the schedule hadn't said, "Water Survival Training: Parachute Drag." At least it was summer and the bay water was warm.

The instructor pointed out that Navy aviators occasionally eject from aircraft in distress, frequently over water. This could be one of us in the near future. Sometimes there is a strong surface wind and we might find ourselves dragged along by a parachute that won't collapse, so we had to learn to get out of our harness while being dragged through the water.

One by one we approached the staging platform. When it was my turn, the instructor and his assistant connected my harness to the hooks and refreshed the procedures they had told the group: "If you're being dragged facedown, give a kick with your right leg and you will flip onto your back, making it easier to breathe." When I was being dragged through the water a moment later, I followed the instructions. It worked! Those who hadn't grasped the lesson were dragged the whole length of the training track. Then they were told to try again. The Navy wasn't trying to eliminate people from the training at this early stage. Later, there would be more serious consequences for failure.

Several days after being dragged by winches, we took another step toward reality. A small boat took us out into the bay and deposited us in the water. Individual life preservers made our wait easier. In a few minutes a CH-46 Sea Knight helicopter dashed out from the shore and noisily approached, its twin blades creating a commotion for ear and eye. It hovered over each bobbing student, lowered a cable, and hoisted the dripping "survivor" about fifty feet to the open side door of the helo. There, a crewman grabbed us and dragged us inside. The pilot deftly moved from student to student, and as we filled the helo one by one, we all smiled and gave each other a big thumbs-up. We weren't sitting in a classroom, and we weren't even in some pool. We were in a big, noisy Navy helicopter, with the door open, and we were almost through with AI.

Our last lesson was a two-and-a-half day survival course. Primitive Navy buses took us to a remote wooded area one hour from NAS Pensacola. We were taught the basics of survival: land navigation, edible plants and animals, and how to make use of available material such as the parachute that we would likely ride to the ground if we did this for real. We land-navigated along courses of three miles or more, ate what little edible foliage we could find, and slept in crude shelters that we built ourselves. When we sat in groups around our fires at the end of the day, we talked about food. That's what hungry people do, and after two days without a proper meal, we were hungry. This modest survival exercise focused on the practical aspects, but later we would deal with survival under hostile conditions.

It was our last week of AI. As a group we didn't know yet that several classmates would not make it through this stage. The selection process was beginning.

I finished number thirteen out of thirty-nine in my class.

For me, the six weeks of AI was a time to transition from seeking a goal to accomplishing it—I had graduated from college, I was commissioned, I was in Pensacola.

I wasn't flying yet, but I was at a naval air station, and all day every day I saw and heard jets.

At the end of AI we were split up. The SNAs went off to other bases to learn pilot stuff like formation flying, aerial gunnery, and carrier landings. Student NFOs, however, simply started attending classes on the other side of NAS Pensacola, known as "Flight Side." We loved just saying it. Flight Side. We also joined our first squadron, Training Squadron Ten. It was a training squadron, but we were in a squadron.

THREE

# Into the Pipeline

Several months before, I was a senior in college. Now I was in a Navy squadron. My full-time job was training for combat in a Navy fighter plane, exactly what I had dreamed, hoped, and prayed for. I had no concept of life in a fighter squadron, but flying in Navy fighters was my only goal, and I eagerly sought each step along the way.

My six-week AI class ended in mid-August. The student pilots then went on to the next level of their training at a base determined by their "pipeline"—that is, whether they would train for helicopters, jets, or props (propeller-driven aircraft such as the P-3, E-2, or C-2). Some pilots went to NAS Whiting, only forty miles from NAS Pensacola in the small town of Milton, Florida, while others went to bases in Mississippi or Texas.

All student NFOs joined Training Squadron Ten on the other side of sprawling NAS Pensacola, near the hangars and runways. In Navy-talk, it was VT-10. Navy aircraft squadrons start with V, a practice that began in 1920 when the Navy selected Z to represent blimp squadrons and V for fixed-wing aircraft squadrons. Don't ask me why. Helicopter squadrons came later; they use the letter H. Squadrons like to give themselves nicknames; VT-10's was Cosmic Cats in 1979, but now it's Wildcats.

To help shape our expectations, instructors explained that most student NFOs would spend ten months in training squadrons: five months of basic flight training in VT-10 followed by advanced training at other squadrons. If we made the grade, those of us who sought fighter seats would then spend about nine months in the F-14 training squadron before arriving at a front-line or "Fleet" F-14 squadron. As we progressed, the aircraft would change from stubby and sturdy subsonic T-2 Buckeyes to world-class F-14 Tomcat fighters. Other details also changed, but many essentials remained constant, such as grade sheets, tests, class rankings, flying with instructors, and the cooperation-competition among students who shared the same goal but knew there weren't enough spots for all of us. Yet most of us needed the support, if not the assistance, of our fellow students to successfully complete training. We weren't clones, but cooperating helped us become a cohesive group. Competition was a climate we all had to live with. We learned that life wasn't fair, and we got used to it.

I had made new friends in AI, and these friendships continued when we went as a group to VT-10. I would eat dinner and hang out at local bars with guys like Paul Rumberger and Steve Jacobsmeyer. Paul and Steve had been friends since they went through thirteen demanding weeks of Aviation Officer Candidate School (AOCS). Immortalized in the 1982 movie *An Officer and a Gentleman* with Richard Gere and Lou Gossett Jr. AOCS turned college graduates into Navy officers by teaching them discipline and teamwork as well as the ability to think on their feet. Paul had attended the University of Florida and was assistant manager at a grocery store when he decided he wanted more adventure. Steve had attended the University of California at Davis and held several jobs, then visited a Navy recruiter on a dare.

I also became good friends with another AOCS graduate, Gary Darby, who had graduated from the University of Texas and sold title insurance for several years. Gary was a mature and friendly guy who didn't know much about airplanes or the Navy, but was in it with all his heart. Fresh out of college, I enjoyed hearing his stories of life in the real world and I appreciated his sincerity and commonsense approach to things.

Some evenings we hung out together at Seville Quarter, a collection of bars and restaurants in downtown Pensacola. Years later, I can still see their young faces—Gary, Paul, and Steve; John Dreswick, Dean Kiyohara, Matt Powers, Henry Smith, Roger Jaskot, John Snedeker, and more. We studied, went to malls, worked out, played softball, and lolled on the beach together. With a group like this it was easy to get three, five, or more guys together to do almost anything. Most of us were single and unattached, so we chased girls, too. With a huge base next to a small town, the guy/girl ratio was distressingly high. We did a lot more chasing than catching.

The Navy offered us many options, and the different personalities in the group had different aircraft as their goal. A few didn't care where they ended up; they knew it would be an adventure. So we were not directly competing with each other at this early stage of training, and we could cooperate and encourage each other while we found our footing in our new Navy life.

We were now assigned to a *squadron*. We went to work at VT-10 instead of the Naval Aviation Schools Command. We wore our bags more often, instead of our khaki uniforms. Our daily activities were controlled by a flight schedule instead of a class schedule. More than instructors and students, a squadron was composed of officers and enlisted personnel divided into departments including maintenance, operations, and administration. They made the squadron run.

The squadron also had a ready room, which was the center of the action for pilots and NFOs. The Squadron Duty Officer (SDO) ran things from the duty desk in the ready room, and was responsible for adhering to the flight schedule. The SDO job rotated daily among the junior aviator pilots or NFOs, those with the rank of lieutenant or below who had been in the squadron at least several months. The SDO had to be savvy enough to keep track of aircraft and people, solve problems in real time, and know which changes to make when changes were required. He was also the direct representative of the commanding officer, a snappy title that showed he was responsible whenever the squadron commander wasn't available. Most of the time the SDO had his hands full with the flight schedule. And if he complained, someone would surely remind him with a grin that SDO duty was "another opportunity to excel."

I found myself in classrooms for a few more weeks, but rather than studying subjects such as aerodynamics and principles of engine operation, we studied aerial navigation and how to conduct a preflight inspection of the aircraft. And now we started training in simulators.

My first simulator was a generic cockpit with rudimentary instruments, known as the 1D23. It allowed me to practice the basics of navigation, communications, and monitoring aircraft instruments. It sounds simple now, but it was challenging at first to follow the established procedures, meet performance standards, and keep track of multiple tasks at the same time.

One of the first new skills we learned was navigating by TACAN, or Tactical Air Navigation. Our basic navigation instrument, the TACAN pointed to a ground station and indicated our distance from it. We could determine our aircraft location relative to the fixed TACAN stations. It just took a little practice.

I started to develop habit patterns and tried to think "ahead of the airplane" to be prepared for what we planned to do next and be ready for possible problems. The 1D23 didn't represent any specific aircraft and had no radar displays or other systems. Its instruments provided only essential flight information such as aircraft heading, altitude, airspeed, and fuel quantity. It was basic, but that was all we were ready for at this stage. Instructors monitored our simulated flights, provided guidance, and graded our performance.

Before coming to Pensacola I had no civilian flight training, the same as most of my fellow students. We had all taken and passed a couple of tests, the Aviation Qualification Test (AQT) and the Flight Aptitude Rating (FAR), which the Navy used to screen both pilot and NFO candidates. The services' preferences and programs change over time, but our instructors told us they would teach us how to fly the way the Navy wanted us to fly.

In one early simulator session we practiced navigating in crosswinds. An airplane flies in an ocean of air, and like the sea, that ocean has currents that we feel as winds. They vary at different altitudes, so that if you watch the clouds on a windy day, you'll often see the low ones moving in one direction and the high ones in another. If you're flying an airplane due north and the air at your altitude is moving due east at twenty knots, that's a crosswind, and it will blow you twenty nautical miles off course in one hour, no matter how fast or slow your plane is flying. Though we would eventually fly in jets with sophisticated navigation computers at more than 600 knots (about 690 miles per hour), we had to learn how to deal with the wind. We had to *understand* how wind behaves, and what it can do if we don't correct for it.

First, an instructor used a device called a navigation computer, similar to a circular sliderule, to explain how to determine wind speed and direction, and then correct for them. Navigation computers are used by aviators in all types of aircraft, and are sometimes called "whiz-wheels." We learned a set of corrections to apply based on our speed and the observed wind effects—how much we were drifting off course. We had each been issued a whiz-wheel to do preflight mission planning, so I just took mine to the simulator and used it to work the navigation problems that we were given. I was getting great results! One of the instructors walking around the simulator room, however, noticed I was using my whiz-wheel to calculate heading changes as the wind changed. He came up behind my chair and pulled my headset away from my ears. I thought he was going to tell me I was doing well, but—*snap!*—he let go of the sides.

Okay, so they didn't want us to use whiz-wheels in the simulator. I got the idea. That drove home the fact that we were supposed to learn the rules-of-thumb, estimate the required correction, apply the estimate, and refine our solution by observing and repeating the process. This fundamental procedural chain remained relevant throughout my training and operational days, from countering the effects of wind to intercepting enemy aircraft.

Through study and repetition, the various correction factors and lessons would become ingrained. In a year I would be flying the F-14 Tomcat, with inertial navigation and a complex weapons system that would perform these calculations. But it was important to learn the principles so we could understand what was going on, plan flights effectively, and deal with the occasional computer malfunction that would be expected when airborne.

## FOUR

# A Down Is Not an Out

Over the course of a month I'd had nine navigation and communication sessions in the generic 1D23. It was time to move up. Now, student RIOs faced the more complex radar intercept simulator, known as the 15C9. We were getting started on becoming a contributing member of the aircraft crew.

In the 15C9 we were introduced to the mission: using our radar to locate a target and verbally direct the pilot to maneuver into position for firing missiles and guns. The hard part was memorizing complex tables of numbers so we could mentally calculate the target's heading, speed, and altitude based on how it moved on the three-inch radar scope. At first the task seemed daunting, especially when I looked at the many charts densely packed with numbers hung up in our classrooms. The instructor stood in front of us and made it clear: "You will be required to *memorize* these charts, then to be able to recall them under stressful conditions, and use that information to direct your aircraft into weapons firing parameters." It was intimidating.

But then I thought: if every other RIO had done it; so could I. My friends and I began to memorize the tables, then worked together to ensure we knew them by heart. We practiced at dinner, while driving or working out, and at local watering holes. And gradually we learned them.

The radar intercept of the 1970s and 1980s was a well-defined series of maneuvers that were based on spatial relationships. When performed by a fighter aircraft, they put it in position to employ weapons against an enemy aircraft. For American fighters of the time, the primary weapons were the AIM-7 Sparrow medium-range missile and AIM-9 Sidewinder short-range missile. The fighter had to manage intercept geometry to arrive within parameters for successful missile launches. Approaching the target, the fighter performed an *attack* to launch the Sparrow from in front of the target, then performed a *counter turn* and a *reattack* to launch the Sidewinder from the rear quarter (see diagram). With a favorable setup and no maneuvering by the target, a radar intercept was a simple challenge for student RIOs. Unfavorable initial positioning, higher speeds, and maneuvering targets—all of which were likely in actual combat—increased the challenge. The introduction of the F-14 in the mid-1970s added the long-range AIM-54 Phoenix missile to the arsenal, but much of the radar intercept remained the same into the 1980s. Things changed when potential enemies fielded fighters with missiles similar to the Sparrow.

In the 15C9 radar intercept simulator, the "pilot" was an instructor who operated dials and switches at a console a few feet from the backseat cockpit mockup. It was fairly simple equipment, so the instructors soon taught students to operate it and allowed us to use it after normal training hours to get more practice. A practice session with a fellow student was known as an extra-time session—an ET. Several evenings a week, my buddies and I would spend an hour throwing setups at each other, trying to apply the memorized values and to think in three dimensions with closing speeds up to 600 knots. That is, your aircraft and the target aircraft flying toward each other, with both aircraft at 300 knots. We constantly reviewed the lessons we were given and quizzed each other on procedures.

In addition to applying the numbers we memorized, we had to perform mental calculations. Here's an example: Determining the target's altitude. You are in your aircraft (or your simulator) flying at an altitude of 20,000 feet above the ocean. Your radar controller identifies a target in front of you at twenty-two miles, but he cannot determine target altitude. You aim your radar in that direction and it takes ten seconds to find the target and put the target in the center of the radar beam—known as "spotlighting." By the time you do this the target is at twenty miles. You check your radar antenna elevation readout and it says the antenna is pointing up two degrees. This may not sound like much, but as you have learned, one degree of antenna elevation equates to one thousand feet of target altitude difference for each ten miles of range. Thus, one degree of look-up at twenty miles is 2,000 feet of altitude. You have two degrees of look-up and the target is at twenty miles so the target is 4,000 feet higher than your aircraft; in this case, the target is at 24,000 feet. Doing the math confirms this:

the sine of 2 degrees is .0349, and twenty nautical miles equals 120,000 feet. Multiply 120,000 feet by .0349 and you get 4,188 feet—close enough. If you're going to shoot the target with a missile it won't be much of a problem, but if you have to intercept and escort it, you will have to climb 4,000 feet.

This was not a job for people who can't do math in their head!

Throughout the months in the two training squadrons, student NFOs concentrated on developing and strengthening skills in these basic skill trainers. Even after we started flying, we would prepare for the next stage of training by performing more complex tasks in simulator sessions.

After graduating from the training squadrons, students reported to a squadron that provided training in the aircraft they would fly in the Fleet, and simulators would continue to be a valuable tool. I hoped to one day be in the Tomcat simulator, which would be quite different from the 1D23 I started in. I knew it would be an accurate reproduction of the F-14 cockpit for both pilots and RIOs. We would practice the most demanding aspects of our mission: fighting multiple enemy aircraft, dealing with seriously degraded systems, and attempting to land aboard a carrier at night—all under a blacked-out Plexiglas canopy in a room with vinyl floor tiles and fluorescent lights. But that was months ahead. In Pensacola I continued to diligently work on the basics.

Classroom, simulator, aircraft. That was the road to mastery of the basic skills. Then it was on to the next skill set, and the cycle was repeated: classroom, simulator, aircraft.

Of course, simulator sessions were graded. On our grading scale, "average" represented an acceptable performance; in this case, it did not equate to mediocrity, but rather to performance as a combat aviator. When I was in a more advanced stage of training for RIOs, I had a stretch of ten sessions over several weeks. My grades were: 4 Above Average, 113 Average, and 8 Below Average, which calculated to a net grade of 4 Below Average. (We could arithmetically compare the Above and Below Average grades for a quick indicator of performance.) That was not very good compared to the other students, but at least I was still in the program. Later in training, I had one of my worst sim days ever. This happened about halfway through the RIO training syllabus, after I had already completed Basic NFO training and had begun flying. I'll tell it here.

I didn't concentrate on some new material I had learned, and essentially I walked into a session unprepared. In this case the intercept geometry was more demanding than before, and the student (yours truly) had to work harder to analyze the spatial picture and tell the pilot (at the console) to make large corrections to intercept the target.

The instructor set up the first run, announcing "Fight's on, your contact is 270 at 28 miles, come right to a heading of 270 degrees." He was playing the part of a radar controller describing an unknown aircraft—a bogey—due west of my position (270 degrees) and 28 miles away. The "pilot" moved the controls to make a right turn to an initial heading of 270 degrees, doing no more or less than I directed. In my simulated cockpit, the compass spun to indicate the turn while my radar display swept back and forth. As we neared the bogey's bearing I observed the target radar blip on the small scope and immediately tried to assess its movement. Remember, this is all in a motionless cockpit replica.

I told the pilot, "Steady up 260 degrees." I could see the blip was slightly left of the original radar call and my command was partly in response to this change, and partly a bluff to say, *I'm in control*.

"Contact 265 degrees, 22 miles, 4,000 feet high, closing," I reported. This was about all the information I could determine from the basic radar we were using at this early stage, and it should have been enough. With no digital readouts, it was a result of observing the small radar scope and performing real-time mental calculation.

Unfortunately, I was already too slow. I was "behind the airplane." The target was drifting and I was not correcting fast enough. I squinted at my radar display and called, "262 degrees, 20 miles, 4,000 high, closure 500 knots." The target had drifted three degrees in two miles. This was a high drift rate based on the tables we'd memorized, and it required a specific correction, but I hadn't studied enough to know the correction. I was using most of my mental capacity just trying to understand the situation, with little left over to figure out how to handle it. I also had difficulty manually adjusting radar antenna elevation to keep the target within the radar beam.

"Come left to 250 degrees." The target return faded from my scope and I had to concentrate on using the thumbwheel on the radar control stick to change the antenna elevation angle and get it back. The situation changed at a rate of one mile every six seconds. I should have ordered a greater heading correction, and should have told the pilot to climb 4,000 feet. It was a reasonable problem that required techniques my class had been taught and had practiced. But for me on this day, it was apparent I had not studied or practiced enough. As the run continued over the next two minutes, I had to order many small adjustments instead of a few effective commands. In the end I did not get in good position to launch a missile.

That first run was ugly, and they didn't get better during my thirty-minute trial. In earlier sessions—when I had been adequately prepared—my instructors had written comments on my grade sheets such as, "Good drift analysis," and, "Well ahead of intercept." But on this day the instructor wrote, "Rear quarter: bad drift control 4 of 5 runs," and, "Terrible, no control of counter turns." The counter turn was the final turn to complete the intercept of the target. Directing one was a basic skill for a RIO. Rear-quarter drift control was another important radar skill for maintaining a positional advantage on an aircraft. The instructor gave me an unsatisfactory grade, a "down," which is equivalent to failing a test. He recommended two supervised ETs and a re-fly of this simulator problem. This got my attention.

During my time in Pensacola it was not too unusual for students to receive a down and continue in the program. It wasn't good, but it wasn't the end of the world either, as long as the student was able to get back on track. And instructors were clear about what it took to be "on track." In the years after I left, I occasionally heard about periods of time when the Navy experienced a backlog in progress from the start of training to the Fleet and would need to eliminate a certain number of students, so even small mistakes were grounds for dismissal from the program. I was fortunate to be there when I was.

I made sure to better prepare for future simulator sessions. I also started keeping a personal notebook recording my performance and lessons learned after each event. As soon as I finished a debrief I would write down major errors or areas for improvement. My early self-criticisms included, "Late altitude corrections," and, "Don't let radar lock difficulties interfere with the run." I kept this notebook well into my Tomcat flying days, and it helped me perform better by developing a mindset of self-improvement. Once in a while I wrote positive remarks, such as, "Pretty good communications."

In addition to the nine 1D23 sessions, I had twenty-three graded sessions in the more complex 15C9. I eventually eliminated my grade deficit, and my final simulator tally when I left Pensacola was a net one Above Average. At least I was in the plus column.

All of this training was to make us ready to *fly*. As we got closer to actually flying, we were introduced to something that would remain familiar for the rest of our flying careers: emergency procedures, or "boldface." Boldface procedures were a specific set of instructions to be followed from memory in the event of a flying emergency. They were so named because they were printed in bold font in the Pocket Checklist (PCL), a five-inch by eight-inch booklet that provided specific information on both routine operations and emergencies for a specific aircraft, such as an F-14 or P-3. Every aviator carried a PCL on every flight. Boldface procedures covered such eventualities as "Engine Fire in Flight," "Loss of Cabin Pressure," and "Uncommanded Control Input." The typical procedure had four to six steps, and the T-2 had dozens of procedures that we learned verbatim.

We all memorized the boldface procedures the same way, by copying them from the PCL onto 3x5 index cards and carrying the cards around for weeks, studying them whenever we had a spare moment. As with radar drift-rate tables, and the other memorization tasks, we tested each other constantly. When VT-10 gave us formal tests on boldface procedures, we had to write them down word-for-word, with no margin for error. All Navy squadrons adhered to this standard. Instructors quizzed us on boldface procedures during the briefing before each flight, and in training squadrons we were quizzed on them during flights. Learning the boldface helped make us fully functioning members of the aircraft crew, and it was just one part of the comprehensive safety program with the unwieldy name, Navy Air Training and Operating Procedures. We called it NATOPS.

The Navy realized it had an aviation safety problem in the 1950s, at which point leadership decided that the current mishap and fatality rates were unacceptable. In 1954, for example, Naval Aviation lost 536 people and 776 aircraft![*] Many changes were put in place to improve this situation, such as training squadrons for each type of aircraft (the replacement air group concept, RAG, which you will read about later) and a culture of safety that included all ranks. One of the changes that affected aviators the most was NATOPS. Launched in 1961, the NATOPS program includes a series of comprehensive flight manuals, one for each type of aircraft, which describe aircraft systems and operating procedures. Aviators are responsible to know the information and required to follow the procedures. The PCL is another component of NATOPS. In recent years the Navy has lost somewhere in the range of ten aircraft or fewer to mishaps each year, which is quite an improvement compared to 1954.

* Figures from Vice Admiral Robert Dunn, USN (Ret.), from his forthcoming book *A Revolution in Naval Aviation*, Naval Aviation Safety, 1950–2000.

(All US military services implemented similar aviation safety programs, with similar results.)

There were many things that could go wrong during a flight, most of them minor. But the emergencies covered by boldface procedures could result in loss of the aircraft if not dealt with quickly and properly. The student—and later, the Fleet pilot or RIO—who did not know and complete boldface procedures during a real airborne emergency displayed a lack of professionalism that was unwelcome at any experience level. It was also dangerous.

Besides boldface procedures, we committed to memory the significant operating limits of the aircraft, such as engine oil pressure limits and allowable gauge fluctuation, maximum airspeed with the landing gear extended, maximum g-force at various aircraft weights, and dozens of other numbers. Again, this knowledge had to be at the forefront of our minds while flying, so we made sure it was, at any time of our days and evenings, while jogging, at bars, during movies. We were informally quizzed on these numbers and formally tested on them. Beyond mere grades, this knowledge sometimes meant the difference between continuing a flight with a minor irregularity or returning to base with an emergency that required the crash trucks to be standing by.

Our instructors didn't need to be dramatic to impress on us the need to learn the boldface procedures and operating limits. We regularly read and discussed mishap reports that told of aviators who dealt with real emergencies. These reports were deeply fascinating. Sometimes we were in awe of a pilot or crew who dealt with scary problems in scary situations, such as flying over ice-cold water at night with almost no fuel or an engine on fire, and successfully making it home. Other times, we couldn't believe a mistake that had been made by aircrew or a controlling authority. Bad advice, misinterpreted information, lack of communication, and dozens of other human errors waited to confound aviators when they least needed confounding. Sometimes it was just bad luck. In every mishap there were lessons, and we worked hard to learn them in the classroom and in the simulator before we climbed into a jet for the first time.

FIVE

# First Flight

The first time I strapped on a Navy jet as a student NFO was in November 1979. It was less than six months after I graduated from college, and those months had been preparation for this day. I was pretty happy with the pace of things so far.

The aircraft was a T-2C Buckeye. It was a Tuesday morning, and we briefed at 7:15. Our callsign for the event was assigned on the VT-10 flight schedule as 0F19. That's "Zero Fox One Niner" in radio-talk.

The T-2 was a dedicated trainer aircraft built by North American Aviation. It entered US Navy service in 1959, and also flew with the Venezuelan and Greek air forces. The T-2 was called Buckeye in honor of the state tree of Ohio, the location of the factory. Powered by two small jet engines, the T-2 was subsonic but sturdy—perfect for training new aviators. The aircraft had a long career with the US Navy, which retired T-2s from training duties in 2008.

My instructor pilot, Lieutenant Roy Lundeen, had flown the A-6 Intruder in the Fleet. Like many experienced Navy pilots and NFOs, he was sent back to a training squadron as an instructor. He had more than a thousand hours of flight time as an A-6 pilot, much of it extremely demanding flying, including low altitude precision bombing in bad weather, aerial refueling at night, and all of the other exciting flying that Navy aviators did routinely. He had earned a great collection of patches, displayed on his flight jacket, and had a great persona for an instructor pilot. He was Jack Nicholson in a flight suit. I got the feeling that he could really mess with students if he wanted to, making the brief and the flight very difficult. But he proved willing to give me a chance and to help me get off to a good start, if I did my part.

*One thousand hours.* Aviators track experience by flight hours. Although it is universally accepted by both military and civilian pilots, this is an inconsistent indicator of experience. The crews of some aircraft accumulate flight time eight hours or more at a stretch, while fighters are in the range of one to two hours per flight. The length of a flight has little to do with its value, anyway. In another year I would learn that burning 16,000 pounds of jet fuel (about 2,400 gallons) in thirty minutes usually provided better training than making that same amount of fuel last two hours. But it's flight hours that we track, brag about, compare, and use as career milestones, regardless of the flaws in this measure. LT Lundeen's one-thousand-plus hours as an A-6 pilot gave him all the credibility he needed.

At 7:15 LT Lundeen and I started going through the briefing guide for flight B-1 (Basic stage, flight number one). It was fairly informal: we sat on a couple of overstuffed brown vinyl couches in the VT-10 ready room and paged through a three-ring binder. Several other student-instructor pairs were also conducting briefings, the SDO was handling phone calls and radio transmissions, and a few students were quietly talking or reading. LT Lundeen didn't insist on formality, but it seemed natural to call him "Sir."

We discussed how the flight would progress, covering the tasks we would each complete as we started the plane and taxied for takeoff, as well as radio and inter-cockpit communications, the training area where we'd be flying, and the maneuvers we would perform. The emphasis was on my duties as a student NFO. To test my knowledge, LT Lundeen grilled me on emergency procedures. "What are the procedures for an aborted takeoff? Engine fire while airborne?" He quizzed me on several of the operating limits. "What is the airspeed limit to fly with landing gear extended? How long can the T-2 fly inverted before the engines are fuel-starved?"

I answered his challenges. Then, trying to establish rapport, I asked him a little about his Fleet experience flying the A-6. He told me a few cool stories. With the capabilities and mission of the A-6, those stories would have impressed even the most seasoned pilots.

Leading up to this moment, I had been through many classroom briefings. Instructors had told us in detail every action required on a flight, and I had practiced in simulators. Now it was a matter of seeing whether I could function in the air. After about forty minutes of briefing we went to the flight gear locker area and got dressed for the flight.

We were already in flight suits for the brief, so in the gear locker (which we also called the paraloft) we had to put on our g-suit, parachute harness, and survival gear, in that order. These were made of nylon and complicated by straps, clips, and Velcro. The first time I got dressed for a flight it took me about twenty minutes to get all of the gear on and adjusted, and I was uncomfortable and hot. I wasn't especially nervous, but I was concentrating.

We stepped into the humid morning air and walked toward the line of T-2s, painted white and orange. These were bright colors for safety, but the US military insignia provided a sense of purpose. The T-2 is not a large aircraft, so when I stood on my toes I could reach into the cockpit. I had to lean down to look into the engines. No one used its official name of Buckeye; instead we sometimes called it "Tubby." But there are worse looking airplanes, and flying the T-2 was a phase all Navy pilots and NFOs went through, so "Tubby" was just fine.

The Student Control Office had given each of us advance notice the week before our first flight was planned. One of the preparations we made was practicing the preflight inspection, or just preflight. This is an orderly and thorough inspection of aircraft panels, wires, pressure gauges, and dozens of other potential problem areas. We would check with the VT-10 Maintenance Control office for an unused jet, then go out to the flight line and spend an hour or so walking around the plane with checklist in hand to learn the procedure. Ultimately, we would preflight the aircraft without referring to the checklist. It required practice and study, and like everything else at VT-10, we were quizzed and graded on what we did.

The volume of information we were required to know was significant. We were learning new facts, new concepts, a new culture. We were tested on all of it. For those committed to flying, this learning process was just another hurdle to clear. Our instructors sometimes reminded us that the lessons were "written in blood," which means that many of the procedures we followed and limits we adhered to were as a result of accidents, sometimes fatal.

LT Lundeen and I were met at the aircraft by our plane captain (PC), a young enlisted man who was responsible for the plane. PCs were among the most junior sailors in a Navy squadron, yet their span of responsibility was significant. They didn't repair the electronics or the engines, but instead performed essential maintenance and inspection checks of the aircraft before and after flights. PCs were directly responsible for ensuring the planes were ready to fly. If the system worked as intended, the aircrew's preflight would be incident-free; confirmation that the plane was ready to go.

We placed our helmets and charts in the cockpit, and for this first flight we performed the preflight together. Walking around the plane we opened panels, peered into engine air intakes, tugged at fuel and oil lines, checked gauges, looked down engine tailpipes, and performed the other required actions. We started on the left side of the plane at the cockpit, walked around clockwise, and returned to the cockpit.

We then climbed the folding ladder on the side of the plane and stepped over the side rails into the cockpit. I directed my foot to the metal floor, careful not to step on the seat cushion lest I leave an oily footprint after walking around on the ramp. The climb up and step down were awkward at first, but the ladder and steps were designed to make the process as intuitive as possible, and after just a few flights I would be manning-up like a pro. At least like a professional student.

The plane captain helped me strap in. The four-point harness would keep a person in the seat during in-flight maneuvers. It would also hold him in the seat during an ejection and would then be his connection to the parachute. I put my helmet on and plugged a combined oxygen and communications link into a connector. I plugged a hose near my waist into the g-suit connector. Once I made all the connections and got a little more settled, things felt pretty much in place, which was amazing considering the complicated flight gear I was wearing. I checked the oxygen flow to the rubber mask, then turned it off until later. To me, bottled oxygen had a "taste" that was somewhat metallic, and combined with the cool rubber of the form-fitting mask it provided a memorable sensation at the start of every flight. On hot days it would come to be a welcome breeze on my face, but I didn't enjoy it on my first few flights.

The PC pulled the last safety pin of the T-2's ejection seat. The pins were metal pieces about three inches long that prevented the ejection seat from firing, keeping the seat safe while the aircraft was between flights. When the PC pulled the last pin, the seat was armed and would eject if the aircrew pulled one of the ejection handles.

I performed my "Pre-Start Checklist," checking the position of all switches in the rear cockpit. They were correct. Occasionally the previous student would leave a switch out of position and the PC would miss it when preparing the aircraft. Sometimes an instructor would place a harmless switch in the wrong position to test the student's alertness.

We knew this was part of the game. At this stage the worst consequence was something minor such as the radio being on when electrical power was applied to the plane, but later we would be in Fleet aircraft with switches that controlled weapons and powerful transmitters, so we performed our procedures with diligence.

LT Lundeen finished his cockpit checks before I did. He was performing actions similar to mine, but his greater familiarity allowed him to work faster. When he switched on the aircraft battery to provide electrical power, we checked our warning lights and checked the inter-cockpit communications system (ICS) that allowed pilot and NFO to talk to each other.

LT Lundeen started the T-2's two jet engines and hand-signaled the PC to pull the electrical power cable from the aircraft. The PC then held his hands up in what resembled a "surrender" gesture. This is the signal for "hands out of the cockpit," so we both stopped what we were doing and put our arms straight out, over the canopy rails, so the PC could see that we were not going to touch any controls. He then checked the hydraulically actuated control surfaces around the aircraft: the speed brakes, flaps, and other devices that controlled the aircraft by their movements. Since they had the power to function at airspeeds up to 500 mph, we could easily break an arm or crush a hand if we moved them while he was checking. We kept our hands and arms clearly visible out of the cockpit. Once this portion of the checks was complete, my job as student NFO became more significant. (Max speed of a T-2 was around 500 mph. Aircraft we flew later would go much faster.)

I turned on the radio and listened to a recorded broadcast that described airfield weather and other information such as the runway on which aircraft were taking off and landing. Many airfields including NAS Pensacola have more than one runway, and as winds change during the day, this broadcast informs aviators which runway is operational.

I switched the radio to the Clearance Delivery frequency and notified a controller that my aircraft would be ready to take off in a few minutes. Clearance Delivery advises air traffic control agencies that a mission on the squadron flight schedule is about to enter the air traffic control (ATC) system. Clearance Delivery also gives the aircrew information such as radio frequencies and instructions for the first stage of flight, immediately after takeoff. To new students trying to copy every word, the call from Clearance seemed like a speed-check for a court stenographer. It was important that I accurately write this information, because I had to read it back to them to confirm that I got it right. Despite the other activity and distractions, I focused and completed the task.

LT Lundeen listened to my radio communications while he completed his checks, then asked over the ICS if I was ready to taxi. Unable to think of a good reason to delay, I said, "Yes, sir!"

He signaled the PC to pull the hard rubber chocks that held the wheels in place. He then added power and we rolled out of our parking space on the VT-10 flight line. It was 8:40 a.m.

I switched the radio to Ground Control. I am certain that all of the other aviators using that frequency could tell it was my first flight as I robotically read into the microphone, "NAS Pensacola Ground Control, Zero Fox One Niner. Taxi . . . IFR . . . Navy Pensacola . . . Information Charlie." Eventually I would know what to say to each controlling agency, but for these first few flights—okay, a few dozen—I wrote every word of expected communication on a 5x7 index card. I kept these cards clipped to my kneeboard, a handy metal plate a little bigger than the index cards, with a large clip at the top and an elastic strap that held it tightly to my right thigh. I think most student NFOs did the same.

Ground cleared us to taxi to the runway, and as we bounced along, LT Lundeen asked me how I was doing.

"Fine, sir."

It required all of my concentration to process the new inputs around me as well as fulfill my responsibilities, so I wasn't able to make more than perfunctory responses to nonessential questions. No idle chatter and certainly nothing clever would come out of my mouth for these first few flights.

The next item on my kneeboard card script was: "Student initiates Before Takeoff checklist." This reminded me to read over the ICS a series of items that had to be completed before takeoff. For each item, depending whether the switch was in the front cockpit or back, LT Lundeen reported his switches were set correctly or I would tell him that I set mine. Our T-2 was now almost configured for takeoff. The most significant item left was our Plexiglas canopy, still raised to allow some air circulation.

The oxygen mask hung from my helmet, attached by one of its two clips. As we approached the runway, I switched on the flow of oxygen and attached the other clip to hold the mask to my face. On early flights the oxygen mask added another new sensation that was a little uncomfortable, but later the mask, along with a lowered visor and flameproof Nomex gloves, would provide a feeling of anonymity and security. I was part of the machine.

Approaching the runway, I gave LT Lundeen a concise description of the departure instructions immediately after takeoff: "For runway 24 Left, fly the runway heading until we are two miles from the TACAN, then turn left to 150 degrees, climbing to 9,000 feet." Having flown from this field hundreds of times, LT Lundeen knew what to do, but this information was good training for the times when I would launch from an unfamiliar airfield. And it was another graded item for me.

As we sat in the hold-short area, I switched the radio to Tower frequency and continued to convey *student!* with every halting transmission.

"NAS Pensacola Tower, Zero Fox One Niner at the hold-short for takeoff . . . IFR . . . time one point two hours." I confirmed the expected flight duration on the schedule, always treating time in hours and tenths.

Tower cleared us onto the runway with a snappy response. "Zero Fox One Niner, position and hold."

With takeoff imminent, we lowered the canopy. After all of my preparation, I felt ready. But talking about something and doing it are worlds apart. I was excited and nervous. I didn't think about the boyhood dreams and the years in college; I thought about the next item on my kneeboard card.

"Standing by with the line up checklist," I announced over the ICS as LT Lundeen used the nosewheel steering to line up our T-2 with the broad yellow and white stripe on the centerline of the 200-foot-wide runway.

LT Lundeen said, "Go ahead," so I started.

"Canopy."

He replied, "Canopy down, light's out," to indicate he had checked the caution light panel. If the light wasn't lit, we knew that a mechanical interlock had been engaged and our canopy was indeed locked into position.

We completed the rest of the checklist.

After a few seconds, Pensacola Tower cleared us for takeoff.

LT Lundeen pushed hard on the tops of his rudder pedals to make the wheel brakes hold the plane. He advanced the two throttles that controlled the aircraft's two jet engines. In back, my throttles moved also. He then performed a control wipeout, moving the stick to its forward limits, then to the left, aft, and right limits to check that he had full range of motion. He had said "Wipeout" before starting, and I turned my head to observe the movement of the ailerons and other control surfaces. I was careful not to impede the movement of the rear cockpit stick as it swirled inches in front of my seat, linked to the control stick in front.

"Ready to go, Dave?"

For the twentieth time I mentally re-checked everything I could think of, then mentally confirmed that the Tower had actually cleared us to take off, and after a half-second said, "Ready!"

LT Lundeen lifted his feet from the pedals to release the wheel brakes, the aircraft nose pitched up slightly, and we were off.

As soon as my airspeed indicator moved, I said, "Off the peg" over the ICS. Doubtless a holdover from the days when a small peg held the indicator at its lower limit, this confirmed our airspeed gauge was working while the pilot concentrated on looking out his windscreen.

A few seconds later, "40 knots," then a few more seconds and, "100 knots." These were standard ICS calls. LT Lundeen made a mental note that I was making them, for my grade sheet after the flight.

As we accelerated, the ride got bumpy. I thought, *Are these tires solid rubber?* The cockpit in the T-2 is large and fairly close to the ground, so there is a good sensation of speed, and a great view. After a few thousand feet of roll, LT Lundeen smoothly pulled the stick aft and we eased into the sky.

*Wow!* I thought for about a millisecond. *My first flight as a student NFO.* It was a milestone, but this was no time for celebrating, so I got back to checking the instruments to be sure I wasn't missing anything.

Shortly after we left the runway I said, "Gear up, flaps up, check transfer on tips." LT Lundeen raised the landing gear handle, raised the lever that controlled the flaps, and moved a switch to command the fuel system to transfer fuel from our wingtip tanks. I watched indicators in my cockpit reflect the changes.

Syllabus flight B-1 had limited objectives. Our mission for this first flight was to get airborne and see whether I could perform basic tasks while flying. It was an early step in the long process of turning a novice into a skilled military aviator. My ultimate assignment was far from certain as far as the Navy was concerned, but in my mind I was on my way to flying F-14 Tomcats off the decks of aircraft carriers.

Checking my kneeboard card, I switched the radio to Departure Control. We turned left to 150 degrees and climbed. For a few seconds we flew over the dense pine woods surrounding the airfield, then crossed roads and a thin strand of beach, and continued out over the Gulf of Mexico. I kept up with the relentless list of tasks and things to say on the radio or the ICS, but I also spent as much time as possible looking outside, at the ground beneath—enjoying a perspective that was endlessly fascinating to me—or at the sky. I was a natural for spotting traffic (other aircraft in our vicinity) because I looked outside so much.

We climbed at 250 knots. It was an overcast day on the ground, but we punched through a layer of clouds at about 5,000 feet, and spent most of the flight among large white clouds in a blue sky.

I switched the radios to the various air traffic control agencies that monitored us as we climbed away from the air station and flew out over the Gulf of Mexico south of Pensacola. Even though he was capable of getting there by himself, at each step LT Lundeen asked me where we should go, and seemed to rely on me to keep our jet inside the assigned training area. It was just a block of air above the ocean, marked on charts by ranges and bearings from the NAS Pensacola TACAN. Before the days of moving maps and GPS it took practice to maintain area control by comparing my actual range and bearing to the airspace boundaries, but like all other student NFOs I mastered the task.

"Want to do some turns, Dave?"

"Sure!"

LT Lundeen rolled 45 degrees left-wing-down and pulled back on the stick slightly while feeding in left rudder. The result was a smooth, level turn at about 2 g.

"How about a loop?"

"Sounds good to me!"

With wings level at 10,000 feet, he pushed the throttles up to military power. The RPM, engine temperature, and fuel flow gauges quickly moved to near the maximum readings on their dials, but unlike a car engine they could maintain these settings for a relatively long time with no ill effects. At 250 knots, he smoothly pulled the control stick back until the g-meter read "4" and our jet began a circle in the sky. Four g is not excessive, and the load decreased as we progressed up the loop. At the top, upside down, we were hanging in our straps for a few seconds. I enjoyed tilting my head back to look at the Gulf of Mexico through the large canopy, then quickly returned to my student NFO duties to check our airspeed and altitude as we started down the back side of the loop. We finished where we started, at 10,000 feet and 250 knots. Good pilots do that.

Throughout the course of the flight our maximum speed was about 350 knots (400 mph), and altitude was 20,000 feet or less. Not spectacular numbers, but zooming around in the sturdy and responsive T-2 wasn't a bad way to fly. It looked tubby but flew well.

Despite the moderate demands on me as a student NFO, the fascinating activity of dozens of instruments, and the vistas of towering clouds and beautiful seas, I hit a speed bump early in my path toward flying fighters. I got airsick!

I said, "Excuse me," to LT Lundeen and turned off the ICS microphone. It was probably a combination of the unfamiliar dynamic motion and the stress of my first flight. Luckily I had grabbed a plastic bag in the paraloft, provided for just this occasion. I put it to use.

When that was over I quickly felt better and was back in action, but thought to myself, *Is this a good way to start a career that will be full of gut-wrenching dogfights and incredible stress?*

LT Lundeen asked if I was doing okay. I assured him I was ready to continue, so we performed more aerobatics. He asked me to do routine tasks and quizzed me on boldface procedures, testing how well I could function in a jet and how well

I'd prepared. Just as I was thinking, *I can do this,* we reached our pre-planned fuel level and had to return to base (RTB). My navigation and communication responsibilities again became demanding as we contacted air traffic control agencies and followed the established routes and altitudes back to NAS Pensacola. At the airfield we did a few touch-and-go landings before the final landing. We cleared the runway and LT Lundeen steered us along the taxiways back to the VT-10 hangar.

We had flown for one hour and fifteen minutes, recorded as "1.3 hours" in our personal logbooks and the documentation for the aircraft. I realized for the first time that I was soaked in sweat. I guess I had been feeling some stress. Even though the g's we experienced were only moderate, they required physical exertion to activate switches, hold my head up and look around, and take notes. It's hard to reach for a switch when it feels as if your arm weighs a ton.

The plane captain directed us to our parking spot and helped us out of the cockpit after we safed our ejection seats by inserting a pin. We went back to the ready room where LT Lundeen debriefed the flight, offering comment and criticism as appropriate. He filled out my grade sheet, marking eighteen specific items such as Headwork, Knowledge of Aircraft Limits, and Communication with Pilot. He graded me 1 Above Average, 16 Average, and 1 Below Average for a net grade of Average.

I was happy. I was exhausted. I got back to my room before noon and slept for four hours.

Over the next few days I talked to my buddies and found that several of them also had occasional airsickness. The instructors told us it was not uncommon, so I continued with determination and envied those lucky students who were never bothered by airsickness. I hoped that I would get used to the dynamic environment. And I did. In the training squadrons in Pensacola, I felt sick or queasy on about ten of my forty flights. This was embarrassing for a hopeful Tomcat RIO, but it was never incapacitating and it became less of an issue as training progressed.

The next day at 6:00 a.m., I briefed for my second flight, and flew for 1.1 hours. I was graded 3 Above, 20 Average, and 2 Below for a net grade of 1 Above Average. Again I was exhausted afterward and took a long nap.

The squadron then took a long weekend for Thanksgiving.

In the next three weeks I had four more flights, including the first stages of training for aerial combat, "basic fighter maneuvers," where instructor pilots in two T-2s maneuvered in close proximity to demonstrate concepts to their student NFO passengers. This was a simple, low-intensity dogfight, and I loved it!

After the first few flights, instructor pilots would occasionally play tricks on student NFOs, in the name of training. One of the most common tricks came just seconds after takeoff: the pilot would comment to the student about unusual clouds, cars in a parking lot, or some other distraction, then intentionally fail to switch the fuel transfer to the wingtip tanks. If the student missed it, the instructor was ready to correct the mistake and point out that such distractions can have drastic consequences. Tricks such as these were reminders that distractions were common and the aircrew had to focus on the essentials. Most students were ready and did not fall for them.

In mid-December I took an out-of-area flight from Pensacola to St. Louis with an instructor who wanted to go home for the weekend, LT Katz. We called such flights cross-country flights, even though we usually didn't fly across the USA, at least at this time. He told me, "I want to go home for the weekend, but this isn't a free ride for you." Flying to another base outside the usual operating area was a great way to gain a lot of experience in a short time, and also a nice fringe benefit.

We left NAS Pensacola early Friday afternoon and landed at the naval air station in Memphis* to refuel, a quick stop known as a "gas and go." From Memphis we flew to Scott Air Force Base in southern Illinois, the nearest military field to LT Katz's home, arriving in the early evening. So in one day I had planned two flights—navigation, fuel, communications, weather, and more—worked with different air traffic control agencies and airfields, and been forced to think and react in real time, away from the familiar Pensacola environment. It was good training.

LT Katz and his family treated me like a welcome guest. He was a licensed private pilot who had flown before joining the Navy, so on Saturday we went to his old airfield and rented a simple Piper Cub to fly around St. Louis. We did not fly under the Gateway Arch; as a local, he knew that was a good way to lose his license. Regardless, for me, buzzing around in that Piper Cub was a great way to see the famous and picturesque city.

On Sunday evening more favorable winds allowed us to fly directly from Scott AFB to Pensacola, a distance of roughly 700 miles. I finished the weekend with some new stories for my young flying career, and a net 1 Above Average. I'm not sure which was more important at the time.

* NAS Memphis was converted to a civilian airport in the 1990s.

SIX

# A Det to the Keys

In January, a storm system developed in the northern Gulf of Mexico and threatened to cost my class a week of training, so on short notice we flew several aircraft to NAS Key West. I had completed 16 flights in the T-2 and my next phase of training at VT-10 involved four flights in the T-39 Sabreliner.

The T-39 was a small jet with two seats up front and a cabin that would seat up to six people. Hundreds of these jets were sold as business jets, and more than one hundred served the military as trainers and small transports. Ours looked like "biz-jets" except for their white and orange paint, national insignia, and four big letters painted on the sides: NAVY. So maybe they didn't look *quite* like business jets. The Navy put a radar in the nose and four scopes in the passenger seating area; they used T-39s to train student NFOs to use the radar for air-to-air or air-to-ground missions, as well as visual route navigation. It was an efficient way to train several students on each flight.

Early one Tuesday morning I climbed into a T-39 with an instructor pilot, an instructor NFO, and two other student NFOs. We had a thick pile of navigation charts and small luggage bags for our four-day detachment, or "det." We left NAS Pensacola under a heavy overcast, but broke into clear weather near Central Florida. We students took turns handling the navigation, communications, and copilot duties as the flight progressed. I was gaining experience and moving from relying on the kneeboard card script to thinking and talking in real time. My grade sheets showed I was making progress.

I was a passenger for much of the flight, as the other students handled the takeoff and mid-flight segments. My turn as a student in the hot seat came on the final portion, as we descended from altitude for a landing at NAS Key West. I coordinated with the instructor pilot to comply with the navigation instructions from air traffic controllers, went through the descent and pre-landing checklists, and switched radio frequencies to talk to the different air traffic control agencies.

We landed and rolled to the end of the runway. For the approach and landing, I'd been in radio contact with NAS Key West Tower, but as we cleared the runway I needed to request permission to taxi to our parking area. This was handled by Ground Control. As we left the runway I confidently said, "Navy Key West Ground, Sabre 91, clear of the duty, taxi to the transient line."

The polite reply: "You're still up Tower frequency, Sabre 91."

Over the ICS the instructor NFO hissed through gritted teeth, "You're embarrassing us."

I switched to the correct Ground Control frequency and repeated my request.

The rest of the det went better.

On that first day I completed three separate flights, more than six hours of flying focused on low-level navigation along established routes. It was valuable experience functioning in a dynamic environment. Just as I had done on my cross-country the previous month, we had to communicate with different air traffic control agencies, not the usual handful we always worked with around Pensacola. We also had to deal with occasional changes to our plans. The det proved to be exceptionally valuable training, as well as an exciting immersion into this still-new environment.

Low-level navigation training was important because combat tactics could demand flying over hostile territory at low altitude. We would eventually fly fighters and bombers with complex navigation systems (at first these were inertial, later GPS), but we had to be able to back up those systems as well as plan the missions. During this det we flew along routes laid out on aviation charts over relatively unpopulated areas of South Florida. With instructor pilots at the controls, we flew 500 feet above terrain at 300 knots (350 mph). We were covering a mile every ten seconds, six miles a minute. Later training flights would bump the speed up to 360 knots. In the Fleet we would go much faster.

A knot is a measure of speed based on the nautical mile, which is 6,076 feet, or about 15 percent longer than the statute mile (5,280 feet) used for most common activities. Speed is measured in knots, which means "nautical miles per hour." One knot is therefore about 15 percent faster than one mph. When you hear "knots," think: *miles per hour plus a little*.

Our training routes were 100 to 150 miles long, which took around 20 minutes at our speed. They usually included six or more "waypoints," landmarks such as power plants, road and railroad intersections, bridges, and other features we could see from the air. During low-levels we were graded on using visual navigation to remain on the route, adjusting course and speed to compensate for the effects of wind, and monitoring fuel and aircraft systems. We also had to update the pilot using standard reports:

Two minutes before each waypoint, the student NFO reported to the instructor pilot something like: "We are two minutes prior to point Charlie. Outbound course will be one eight five degrees, recommended altitude is six hundred feet. Point Charlie is the railroad bridge over the river that is coming up on our left side." (The 600-foot outbound altitude would keep the aircraft at 500 feet over terrain or obstacles that were 100 feet above sea level. This part of Florida was near sea level, but occasionally we had a building or structure along our route.)

Passing over the waypoint, we made a mark-on-top report: "Mark! Turn left to one eight five. Time is seven-plus-one-five, we are three seconds late." At jet speeds, seconds do count; we were almost half a mile behind.

Once the aircraft rolled wings level after completing the turn, the student reported: "Wings level, heading is one eight five degrees, airspeed is three hundred knots, altitude is six hundred feet. We have two thousand five hundred pounds of fuel, which is as planned. We were on top of point Charlie at seven-plus-one-five, which is three seconds late, no correction required. In one minute there will be a radio tower seven hundred feet high, two miles right of centerline."

And on it went throughout the route. Low-level flying demanded thorough preparation. I looked up the specifications for the route in a reference book that listed all low-level training routes in the United States, then prepared detailed charts with numerous notes, which would support my in-flight commentary. I then studied the route before the flight. During the flight I had dozens of conditions and instruments to monitor. I had to think ahead of the plane, observe, and talk all at the same time. It was exciting and fun. With a great view of the countryside rushing past, we flew fast enough to require concentration, but a good student could keep up. And when I commanded corrections to heading, speed, or altitude I could see the effects in a few seconds. The instant feedback was an effective reward.

On the second day of the Key West det I had to demonstrate some flexibility. The first student sat in the right seat in the cockpit for the takeoff and a low-level route, while another student and I occupied the T-39's cabin waiting our turns. An instructor pilot always flew the jet from the left seat. For us in back it was a great opportunity for a mental dry run. Then the second student went up front and took his turn at navigating, while the first student and I exchanged comments about how the flight was going.

Finally it was my turn to direct the flight, so I took my chart and sat in the right-hand seat up front. It went well. But near the end of the route we found ourselves lower on fuel than expected, and decided to divert to the small municipal airport at Vero Beach on the Atlantic Coast of Central Florida. I was excited—a real-time change of plan! The instructor pilot and NFO coached me and we landed without drama.

One of the good things about flying in a plane designed as a biz-jet was that it could be serviced almost anywhere. We had the jet refueled, grabbed a little food, and set off for another round of low-levels on the way back to Key West.

After the last flight of each day we finished debriefing, got our grade sheets, discussed the plan for the next day, and got a quick dinner. Then the instructors headed out for cold beers while the students got together and made charts for the next day's flying. It was intense, great training, and tiring, and we all enjoyed it.

My grade sheet from the last flight of the det included the instructor's comments: "Very confident (maybe too much), but should do well." At this point I was carrying 10 net Above Average out of about 370 graded items on all of my actual flights—not a world record but a strong performance.

I got back to Pensacola late Friday morning. That afternoon my friend Ray Para and I jumped into his 280Z for the six-hour drive to Atlanta. We had been pals for four years at Georgia Tech and Ray had recently arrived in Pensacola for AI, along with another classmate and friend, Ted Rogers. We still had a lot of friends in Atlanta and it was a favorite weekend road-trip destination.

When I returned to Pensacola on Monday my class completed VT-10. There was no "graduation," just a short gathering in a classroom to receive our completion certificates.

Up to this point, two guys out of my class left the aviation program and transferred to other communities to serve their military obligation. One was assigned to a submarine, the other was a Marine Corps officer who joined Marine ground forces. We all knew these guys weren't doing too well with us. For their part, they seemed to have decided they really didn't want to fly. We expected to lose a few along the way. Flying isn't for everyone.

Several other students had already separated from the class to begin the training pipeline for the P-3 Orion, and others now left for E-2 Hawkeye training. The missions of these aircraft placed specialized requirements on their NFO crewmembers, so they continued flight training in their own pipelines at different bases. Guys like Henry, Dean, John, and Roger—my friends for 4-5 months—broke away to get on with their training. I never saw most of them again.

At our final class meeting I learned that I ranked number two among the nine students in my VT-10 class. More important, I was officially selected to enter the RIO syllabus for the next phase of training, which meant I was going to fly fighters. As much as I respected the other aircraft in the Navy's arsenal and the committed aircrew who flew them, my personal goal remained flying the F-14 Tomcat as a radar intercept officer. Paul and Steve also received their preference, which was to continue on to RIO training. Other friends began the attack syllabus as they requested, and a few were detailed to training for aircraft they did not request. The explanation was simple: needs of the Navy. Some learned to enjoy the work they were assigned, while others served their time and moved on. But since this was the military, we all served our time at the very least.

The next level of training after VT-10 was VT-86, which had a syllabus for students destined for fighters and another for those destined for attack aircraft (at the time, the A-6, EA-6, and S-3). VT-86 was located next to VT-10, and the atmosphere and pace were similar: classes, simulators, flights with instructors, and grade sheets. But it was focused on the mission the student would ultimately perform. VT-86 was known as the Sabrehawks, since they flew the T-39 Sabreliner and TA-4 Skyhawk.

My final VT-10 event was on a Monday morning, and Tuesday morning at 7:30. I was scheduled for my first event in VT-86. Arrival at the new squadron was anticlimactic. For various reasons we didn't have enough students to justify starting a new class for RIO training, so we were told to wait two weeks until another VT-10 class graduated and provided more student RIOs. This was not unusual. Meantime, we were in a *pool*, available for various duties on short notice. In our case, we checked in once a week. The Pensacola weather was terrible, so I seized the opportunity for a trip to my hometown of Jacksonville.

SEVEN

# We Joined the Navy to Fly!

Our VT-86 classes started on February 6, and the emphasis was on radar intercept procedures, which would be a large part of our duties as RIOs whether in peacetime or in combat. This was where we met the more detailed simulators I mentioned earlier.

After some introductory simulator time, our instructors were eager to get us back in the air. And so were we. We joined the Navy to fly!

The flying portion of the VT-86 syllabus started with the same T-39 aircraft we had used in VT-10, only the student NFO now used the radar to track an aircraft target and direct an intercept. The procedures were identical to those I had been using in the simulator, but the ambiance was quite different. The student sat in the cabin and used the radar to direct the instructor pilot to intercept the target. Meanwhile, two or three other students waited, listening with headsets and watching repeater radar displays. We usually had the window shades pulled down to make the scopes easier to see, so it was dark. The student doing the directing frequently made mistakes, resulting in necessary adjustments of the T-39's turn, altitude, or airspeed—often reversing a move commanded only seconds before.

It was a rough ride, and with the shades down we could not see the horizon and clouds sweeping up and down outside, but we could feel it in our stomachs, and that's a classic cause for seasickness and airsickness. Sometimes even the seasoned instructor RIOs were stretched out on the aircraft floor between runs, trying to re-establish equilibrium. By this time I was no longer getting sick, but sometimes had to contend with bouts of queasiness. I still hoped that having an unobstructed view of the sky, as provided by the Plexiglas canopy of an F-14, would solve this little problem. I *hoped*.

Despite the challenges our new training presented, we continued to find opportunities for road trips. The long Easter weekend came two months after I started VT-86, so Gary and I planned a trip to Austin, Texas, where he still had many friends from his days at the University of Texas, Austin.

We left on Thursday. But first I had a date with a simulator that began at 5:45 a.m., so my day started early. Later I had a class meeting at 1:00 p.m. Gary had scheduled events, too, but we finally got on the road in the late afternoon. We were traveling in style in Gary's brand-new 1980 Chevrolet Monte Carlo, but those were the days of the 55 mph speed limit, and it took us more than twelve hours to make the 685-mile trip. When we arrived at Bergstrom Air Force Base (AFB), just outside of Austin, we had both been awake more than twenty-four hours, so we checked into rooms in the visiting officers' quarters and got some rest.

However, friends were waiting, so we didn't nap long. Soon we were headed to the University of Texas campus. Gary's friends were excited to see him and hear about his flying adventures, and they welcomed me as one of their group. The Eagles album *The Long Run* had recently reached #1 and we listened to it on cassette as we visited their favorite restaurants and bars. It was a great visit, but we had to get back, so we got on the road early Sunday afternoon. The return drive seemed longer than the trip over, and we reached Pensacola around 4:00 a.m.

Fortunately my only event on Monday was a "phone muster." I had to wake up to call the squadron at 8:00 a.m., then I went back to sleep. During times like this with few scheduled events, Gary, Paul, Steve, other classmates and I made sure we practiced our radar intercept numbers and took ET sessions in the trainer when we could.

By mid-April, two months after starting training in VT-86, I had completed nine flights and was carrying a net 3 Below Average: 5 Above, 137 Average, and 8 Below. While privately I was disappointed that I wasn't doing better, I was staying solidly in the program and appreciated some of the comments on my grade sheets, such as, "Nice job in spite of many small screw ups."

But my flaws were accumulating. It seemed I was missing some basic understanding and probably could have used more practice, because on Tuesday afternoon, April 15, I received a "down" for my performance during a flight. The performance objectives were logical next steps in my training, and I had completed the classes and preparatory simulator sessions. My task was to obtain radar contact on a single target, analyze the movement of the radar blip, and direct my aircraft into a firing position.

I knew real-time that my performance was lacking, but the magnitude of the problem became clear in the debrief after we landed. The instructor's comments on my grade sheet indicated fundamental problems: I wasn't adjusting the radar correctly to paint the target and was slow on controlling the intercept. These were things I had practiced in the simulator and that my classmates were doing, so there was no excuse. My performance wasn't up to standards, so I had to appear in my white uniform before a board of three instructors, to be convened three days later on Friday afternoon at 1:00.

At the same time, some excitement was developing outside of my flying activities. In the weeks before this flight, one of my instructors had noticed my pristine '72 Mustang convertible and said he was thinking of getting a classic like mine. We had talked about the car several times and discussed trading cars for a weekend. He had a one-year-old Corvette, so I jumped at the chance. I'm sure it wasn't a factor, but the day before I got my down grade we agreed to trade cars the next weekend.

Rather than daydreaming about the car-swap, I spent the days before my review board appointment nervously going over all of the information they had taught me and trying not to panic. I was only able to get one simulator ET. I talked to other students who had received downs. Most of the input I got was encouraging: if you knew your stuff, were committed to the program, and took the board seriously, you would probably get thumbs-up to continue. I knew the essential material and was functioning in the plane fairly well. I was definitely committed to the program. I had no trouble taking the board seriously as I thought of classmates who had already been cut from the program, and I had no desire to serve out the remainder of my commitment to the Navy exiled to a destroyer or at some remote base. But as hard as it was for me to grasp, being kicked out of flight school was definitely an option.

At the appointed time on Friday I stood before three instructors at a Progress Review Board. They were in their khaki uniforms; I was in the more formal whites. It was set in a warm classroom, and they sat behind a long table, which conveyed the seriousness of the proceedings. Fortunately they allowed me to take a seat. They asked me questions about the aircraft, operating the radar, intercept procedures, even administrative questions about my training record. I didn't get all of the answers right, but I got most of them, and I conveyed my commitment to becoming a fighter RIO. All three board members voted to allow me to continue my training after some remedial training sessions.

I felt a profound sense of relief. I couldn't even imagine being derailed from my career aspirations at this time. But being twenty-one years old has its benefits, such as being able to feel like I could easily dodge a bullet and take it in stride. Moments after the board voted to allow me to continue, I was looking for my instructor friend who wanted to swap cars. We traded keys and I left the VT-86 parking lot in a nearly new Corvette, mine for the weekend.

Five minutes later I arrived at my room in the bachelor quarters as my roommate Gary was hanging up the phone. "That was Ray and Ted. They want to go to Atlanta. I told them to wait for us." Gary knew about my car swap and was ready for a Corvette road trip.

Ted and Ray had completed their six weeks of AI at NAS Pensacola and had started pilot training forty miles away at NAS Whiting Field. Normally, they would have left for Atlanta immediately and we would meet them there, but Gary told them to wait. He just didn't tell them why. A 1978 Corvette cost about $10,000, which was roughly a year's salary for me and my ensign friends, so it was a thrill to have the car for a weekend. It was great to see the look on Ray and Ted's faces when Gary and I drove up to their quarters in that Vette. Then we headed for Atlanta, Ted driving his car and Ray in his. We stuck together on the drive up, and in those cool wheels, the trip seemed to take less time than usual.

In Atlanta we checked in with as many old friends as we could find around Georgia Tech. Some were underclassmen, others were in graduate programs. I think I forgot to mention to some of them that I was just borrowing the car.

EIGHT

# Navy Wings of Gold

When we returned to Pensacola I had less than two months left at VT-86. By this time in my training, most weeks I only had a few scheduled events and was expected to spend free time studying. Summer came early in Pensacola, and I often took my course material to Pensacola Beach where I studied on the sand (when not distracted). As the days heated up, the squadron scheduled flight ops as much as possible in the morning when it was cooler. Sometimes my day started early to make a 5:00 a.m. briefing, but that meant I could be on the beach before noon. I finally had a solid understanding of the material and was feeling comfortable in the aircraft. The instructors still didn't give anyone a free ride, but I was actually enjoying the training.

My flying syllabus consisted of eight more flights in the T-39, in which I made steady progress, and six flights in the TA-4 Skyhawk, a nimble two-seat training jet derived from the single-seat A-4 light bomber.

Developed in the mid-1950s, the A-4 provided the Navy and Marine Corps with a versatile aircraft that could be operated from aircraft carriers. It had been used extensively in Vietnam and was flown by a half-dozen foreign forces. At the time I was training, the Navy's famous flight demonstration team, the incomparable Blue Angels, flew A-4s. The TA-4 version included a second seat with complete flight controls, and hundreds of them were used to train student pilots and NFOs. The A-4 was a simple design compared to most US military aircraft, yet proved its versatility over a career that lasted until 2003 with the US Navy. At the time of this writing, A-4s continue to serve with several foreign forces and private operators in the United States.

Student NFOs were happy that our syllabus included some TA-4 flights because they involved dynamic maneuvering in close proximity to another TA-4, which gave us a chance to experience the dogfight portion of the fighter mission. Although prognosticators had predicted since the late 1950s that air-to-air-missiles would bring an end to the dogfight, combat experience had proven them wrong. Missiles sometimes failed and the enemy sometimes sneaked up on you. Dogfighting remained an essential skill for fighter pilots, and as prospective RIOs we would have to perform as part of the fighter crew during the fight. Our TA-4 flights were a nice finish after months of looking at radars and crunching numbers.

The TA-4 was the sleekest jet we had flown thus far. For these flights we always took off and flew to our training airspace in formation with another TA-4, which also carried an instructor pilot and student NFO. Instead of the dark cabin of the T-39, I once again enjoyed an amazing view through a Plexiglas canopy. Painted white and orange like the T-2 and T-39, the TA-4 looked great zooming through the bright blue skies off Pensacola, which were populated with puffy white clouds this time of year.

During the maneuvering portion of the flight we were opponents. The action always started with the same radio call: *fight's on*. Each jet would try to out-fly the other, with specific training objectives and clear safety rules helping to prevent these flights from becoming ego-fueled fights to the finish. The dogfight ended with a distinctive radio call, too: *knock it off*. We would then get set up for the next event, such as another dogfight where one jet started in a position of advantage. These flights consisted of five or six specific events, called *engagements*, and then our training objectives were met. For the flight home, one TA-4 again flew as the wingman and returned in tight formation on the lead aircraft. The student NFOs in both jets had specific duties depending on whether they were lead or wingman.

With no comparable experience beforehand, tactical maneuvering could have been a brain-scrambling and unpleasant way to fly. But we'd had excellent orientation classes in the principles behind aerial combat and how they affected our flight. This was the culmination of lessons I had learned over the past ten months.

Gravity, for example. The abstract concept was now very real as it affected how we would move the controls throughout a vertical loop. And we saw how the g's we pulled in a horizontal turn affected the aerodynamic drag on the aircraft. Since drag was the countering force to the thrust of the engine, the pilot had to carefully balance his maneuvering and his engine power. Throughout the fight, the RIO had to know what to expect and how to make himself most valuable. Building on the classroom sessions, my instructor pilots did a great job of talking me through the demonstration phases and then coaxing my participation.

The later flights included a segment where each student RIO "called the fight," the instructor pilots in the front seats becoming remote-control pilots following their student RIO's commands. I stuck to the basics. "Roll right. Hard turn. Steady up, Roll right and go nose low. Now loop!"

During this phase there was banter on deck about whether someone's pilot was actually making the decisions during the RIO-called engagements, or which student RIO was the best. Challenges were made and bets were placed. We students were anticipating the completion of training and enjoying the sense of accomplishment. For the instructors, who went through this phase every two weeks, the familiarity made it no less enjoyable as they prepared to send the latest class forward into the Fleet.

If you think calling the flight sounds fun for us, instructors also gave student NFOs some stick time. At points where we couldn't get into too much trouble, such as once the jet was at altitude and we were transiting to the assigned operating area, the instructor might say, "Do you want to fly it?" Of course I always said, "Yes!"

"You've got the jet," he said, ensuring positive transfer of control.

The stick grip was front and center, a hard piece of plastic sized and shaped to feel comfortable to the grip; it felt natural in my right hand. The throttle, which controlled engine speed, sprouted from the left console, placed for easy control with my left hand. Clearly aircraft cockpit designers had learned many lessons about ergonomics before I even climbed into a cockpit. But the natural feel didn't do much to help my ham-fisted control, based on no experience: it takes a light touch to move a jet, especially a responsive machine like the TA-4. If you "tried" to fly straight and level, you would probably mess up. The trick was to relax, but that is hard to do during your first few minutes of actually flying.

My instructor pilot said, "Let's try a full-performance roll. Throw the stick hard to the left." Its high roll rate was one of the TA-4's notable features. So I pushed the stick to the left and we did a halfhearted roll, the earth and sky tumbling outside my cockpit, until we were upright again and I centered the stick.

My pilot said, "Not bad, but let me fly for a second and I'll show you what she'll really do."

"You've got it," I said

With that, the control stick *snapped* to the left and we completed a roll in less than a second, returning upright as we had started. I gasped, "Wow, that's amazing!"

He gave me the controls, I tried again, and got closer to his demonstration of the maximum roll rate. We performed a few other simple maneuvers and then it was time to get back to the scheduled syllabus. These brief experiences at the controls were priceless, giving us a small sense of what our pilots were doing. When we went to our fighter squadrons we would not have this opportunity, as Navy fighters (F-4s and F-14s) did not have control sticks in the backseat.

My final flight in a TA-4—my last flight in the Training Command—was graded 9 Average and 2 Above Average.

The instructor's comments were, "Nice job as lead; very smooth hop. Comm lead was excellent. No mistakes." That Progress Review Board had not voted wrong.

On Friday, June 13, 1980, in a ceremony at the new Naval Aviation Museum, I received my coveted Wings of Gold for successfully completing the Naval Flight Officer training program. That Friday the 13th was certainly a lucky day for me!

Navy Pilot wings are about 2¾ inches wide, with a shield and fouled anchor in the center. The current design used today is an evolution of the original, which dates to 1917. NFO wings are the same size and similar in appearance, but have two anchors, crossed. The term NFO and the wings were approved in 1968, replacing earlier designations and insignia. All NFOs wear the same wings, regardless of their aircraft.

These gold wings were a tangible symbol of accomplishment, a result of hard work and some good fortune. I would soon find out that they also stood for adventure, service, responsibility, danger, and exhilaration. But I wasn't thinking of any of that. I was caught up in the moment. The winging ceremony was a blur of activity, as fifteen of us graduated that day, with wives, girlfriends, parents, family, and friends watching proudly. There was enough ceremony to make it impressive, but not pompous. Besides, we all wanted to hit the Officers' Club and celebrate. And celebrate we did! Fortunately I had a designated driver.

In the days before graduation, instructors had asked my duty preference. I requested "F-14s, East Coast," which would have been an assignment to NAS Oceana in Virginia Beach, Virginia. As often happens in the military, I didn't get exactly what I wanted. When they read my orders at the graduation ceremony, I heard, "F-14s, West Coast," which meant NAS Miramar, San Diego, California. I didn't think about Topgun, clear skies over the desert, wide airspace over the Pacific, living in San Diego, trips to Hawaii, or deployments that would take me to Chinese Hong Kong, Australia, and Africa. But it only took me a half-second to realize I was happy. My friends Paul and Steve got their wings the same day and also received orders to F-14s West. Gary was a class behind us and received his wings two weeks later. He got orders to F-14s West, too.

I'm gone! I packed my meager belongings, jumped into my Mustang, and drove across the country to San Diego with the top down most of the way. I put on my flight helmet a few times, which probably looked stupid, but at this point I didn't care. I had so much enthusiasm and felt everything was happening the way I dreamed. I was twenty-one years old and about to start F-14 training.

## Aircraft Specifications and Designations

Does life get any better than that? Yes, it does! Compare what I'd flown so far to the Tomcat waiting for me up ahead:

| | T-2C | T-39D | TA-4J | F-14A |
|---|---|---|---|---|
| Nickname[1] | Buckeye | Sabreliner | Skyhawk | Tomcat |
| First flight[2] | 1958 | 1958 | 1954 | 1970 |
| Length | 38 ft, 8 in | 44 ft | 42 ft, 7 in | 62 ft, 9 in |
| Wingspan[3] | 38 ft, 2 in | 44 ft, 4 in | 27 ft, 6 in | 64 ft (spread)<br>38 ft (swept) |
| Takeoff weight | 13,000 lbs | 20,000 lbs | 20,000 lbs | 62,000 lbs |
| Maximum speed | 460 knots<br>(521 mph) | 440 knots<br>(500 mph) | 574 knots<br>(660 mph) | 1,340 knots<br>(1,544 mph) |
| Service ceiling[4] | 44,400 ft | 43,100 ft | 38,700 ft | 50,000 ft |

Notes:

1. Aircraft are listed in the order I flew them. Data for the T-2C, T-39D, and F-14A came from the US Navy website. Data for the TA-4J came from www.aero-web.org.
2. First flight of the first aircraft in the series. For example, 1958 was the first flight of the T-2A, the original variant of this type as indicated by the "A" after the number. The T-2C that I flew had two engines instead of the single engine in the A, and it entered service in 1968.
3. The Tomcat's wings are movable, spread straight out for maximum lift at takeoff, landing, and maneuvering, swept back for speed.
4. Ceiling is defined as the highest altitude at which an aircraft can still meet specified performance parameters, usually the rate of climb.

Aircraft designations were made according to a system. The F-14A, for example, can be decoded as follows: First letter, F, meant fighter. Other common types in US forces are: A—attack; B—bomber; C—cargo; E—electronic mission; K—tanker; P—patrol; T—trainer; X—experimental. Letters can be combined, so that F/A is a multi-mission fighter and attack aircraft, and TA is a trainer variant of an attack aircraft.

The number is based on a sequential numbering of aircraft of that type. The same number can be used in different mission categories; the T-2 and C-2 are a trainer and cargo plane, respectively.

The final letter refers to the version in this case the F-14A was the initial type produced. Later the Navy also used F-14Bs and F-14Ds.

These conventions could be modified. For example, giving into superstition there was no F-13.

Most US aircraft also have names, and some notes on these can be found in the Glossary.

NINE

# Ants, Tomcats, and American Pigs

I took the long way across the country and enjoyed the trip. Passing through Los Angeles at rush hour—L.A. traffic was heavy and fast, even back in 1980—I arrived at Miramar on a warm Thursday evening and officially checked into the F-14 training squadron, VF-124.

Thirteen months after graduating from college, here I was, on the threshold of flying Tomcats for a living. At times, the requirements and milestones had come at a challenging pace; at other times it was almost relaxing. I felt things were going well. The Navy did a good job of tracking my expectations with charts that showed typical career progress. I knew roughly how much time I would spend in each major stage of training, how long I would spend in my first Fleet squadron, and so on. I didn't really study these charts, though. I was superstitious about trying to plan for something I wanted so much. But the information was available when I needed it. I was usually looking just several days ahead, and that seemed to be working for me.

I checked in to VF-124 after working hours and was told by the sailor on duty that my class would start Monday at 8:00 a.m., so I had three days to kill. The next day I joined up with Paul, who arrived a few days before me. Steve was visiting family and friends in Redondo Beach, two hours north of San Diego, and would arrive in a few days. We would be in the same RAG class. Gary and other buddies from Pensacola would arrive in the coming weeks.

VF-124's squadron name was the Gunfighters, but everyone called it "the RAG." That stood for Replacement Air Group, an old designation that had been officially changed in 1963. The new term was FRS for Fleet Replacement Squadron, but the RAG nickname stuck. All squadrons that trained aviators in Fleet aircraft were called RAGs. VF-124 was the West Coast F-14 RAG, while the East Coast F-14 RAG was VF-101 at NAS Oceana in Virginia Beach. There were RAGs for the A-6, P-3, S-3, and others, at least one RAG for every major type of aircraft the Navy flew.

We were in a new environment. After becoming completely familiar with Pensacola—after the sense of accomplishment that came with our Wings of Gold—we were again "freshmen," but this time in the Real World. We were in a training squadron, but it was a *Tomcat* training squadron. A *combat* squadron was adjacent to us in the hangar; we were that close. The F-14s, F-4s, and RF-8s we saw flying were a purposeful gray instead of the safety-painted white and orange trainers we were used to. These fighter aircraft were louder, they used afterburner for takeoff, and they sometimes carried missiles and bombs. There weren't a lot of young ensigns running around the base—we were now outnumbered by seasoned lieutenants, lieutenant commanders, and higher-ups in the pecking order. They had been on long overseas deployments, intercepted Soviet bombers trying to sneak up on our carriers, shot missiles, had friends who had died in plane crashes, escaped death themselves. I was even surprised to see Bill Driscoll there, an ace with five MiG kills as an F-4 RIO during the Vietnam War.* I read about him when I was a teenager studying airplanes while my friends "studied" baseball, and now he was one of my RAG instructors. Almost everyone on Miramar had great stories, and I was rarin' to start creating stories of my own.

VF-124 was a lot like VT-10 and VT-86 in many respects. I was a student, and of course the instructors were seasoned and savvy. Flying the F-14, using the AWG-9 weapons system, and training for combat missions would be even more exciting than what I had experienced in Pensacola. The simulators we would now train in were accurate reproductions of F-14 cockpits. But I was still being graded on almost everything, taking written tests, and memorizing huge volumes of information.

The differences soon became even more apparent. Some of our lectures were classified, meaning that we needed security clearances to hear them, we could not discuss

* In 1972, Bill Driscoll, as a lieutenant (junior grade)—a relatively junior officer—flew as RIO with LT Randy Cunningham on combat missions over Vietnam in which they shot down five enemy "MiG" fighters, earning them the unofficial title of aces. They were the first US aces of the war, and were followed by an Air Force pilot, Captain Steve Ritchie, and two Air Force backseaters, Captains Charles DeBellevue and Jeff Feinstein. All of the kills were scored while flying F-4 Phantoms.

the material outside of secure areas, and we had to leave any study material in a classified storage area. No more reading training manuals on the beach. Material was classified because it dealt with specific weapon capabilities and detailed tactics. All material that we had studied in the training squadrons was unclassified. Dealing with classified material was exciting, but it was also a big responsibility.

Another difference was that we trained alongside student pilots. During my year of NFO training, all students and many instructors were NFOs, outnumbering pilots, who flew the jets of course and taught several classes. Now we NFOs found ourselves in roughly equal numbers to our pilot brethren. Pilots in RAG classes were in a similar situation, having been through two years of training with no NFOs. Since we were in fighters, NFOs were now RIOs. The pilots also got a special name: fighter pilot. Classes included pilots and RIOs together, but for most flights, two students would not fly together. Student pilots had instructor RIOs in their backseats, and student RIOs flew with instructor pilots up front.

When I reported to VF-124 on Monday morning I discovered that my class included a pilot named Sandy Winnefeld, who graduated from Georgia Tech the year before I did, and also had gone through Navy ROTC. We were now in the same class because pilot training took roughly a year longer than NFO training, in part because pilots had to accomplish demanding carrier landings while they were students. It was great to have a fellow Georgia Tech alumnus in my class.

Like most RAG classes, mine also included seasoned fighter pilots and RIOs who were returning to the community after a tour doing something other than flying fighters, such as working in the Pentagon. They took a refresher course that was shorter than my training, which was for people new to the F-14. We had several lieutenant commanders: pilots, and RIOs who seemed to me to be as experienced as Chuck Yeager himself. They were all exceptionally helpful to us neophytes, doubtless recalling their own bewilderment years before.

And so began VF-124 class 8007, the seventh class of 1980.

A few days after joining the RAG, Paul and I were hanging around the ready room, getting a sense of the place and listening to great flying stories, when we decided it was time to start learning how to preflight the F-14. We checked with Maintenance Control for a jet we could climb on. Maintenance was used to us ensign students, and directed us to a jet in the hangar that had a lot of panels unhinged for troubleshooting and repairs. It wasn't going anywhere for the foreseeable future.

Like most carrier-based aircraft, the Tomcat had a short ladder that unfolded from the left side of the fuselage below the cockpit. It provided the first steps up, leading to push-in panels on the fuselage for handholds when you were climbing up, and steps when you got there. At the top there were two small foldout platforms that the pilot and RIO stood on to get in and out of their cockpits.

I slowly threaded my way up the ladder and negotiated these new climbing aids, hugging the jet as I climbed. On the top foldout panel I was standing almost ten feet off the ground. I took the short step to the top of the engine intake, then stood on the top of the jet, a gently curving surface that seemed huge.

In my khaki uniform, hands on my hips, I surveyed the gray upper surface of the jet. It conveyed power and speed even though it was smudged with greasy footprints and had several missing panels. I tried to act like I belonged, though I sure didn't feel like it.

In a few months I would be familiar with every panel and contour, aware of every antenna waiting to be kicked and broken, and cautious of every fragile cooling vent to be avoided, lest it be crushed by the careless flight boot. But for now I carefully walked around on top of the jet for a few minutes. Paul and I found most of the inspection items that we would soon be required to check on preflight, at first for the sake of a grade sheet as well as our own safety. And then we decided to get down before we fell or did something stupid.

In addition to RAG classes I spent a few weeks renewing some quals and gaining new ones. I was picked up by a helicopter in San Diego Bay, took another simulated ejection seat ride, and spent many hours in large swimming pools, usually wearing a flight suit and boots, and sometimes a helmet.

For us new guys the first really significant experience was SERE School, named for the survival, evasion, resistance, and escape techniques we learned in case we fell into enemy hands. The Army, Air Force, Marine Corps, and Navy all conduct SERE programs to help prepare personnel who would be susceptible to capture by enemy forces during combat operations (combat ops). The Navy required all carrier-based aviators and several other groups to complete SERE training.

My weeklong SERE class began with two days in a large Navy classroom at NAS North Island, across the bay from downtown San Diego. We were about forty young men, mostly officers plus a few enlisted aircrewmen. (Women did not yet fly combat aircraft, and thus were not required to complete SERE training.) Paul and Steve were in my class. On Thursday and Friday we had lectures on SERE and prisoner of war (POW) concepts, and the specific training we would soon begin. Saturday was a day off. Sunday morning we began the field portion of training.

Breakfast before class on Sunday was our last regular meal for more than four days. After lectures on how to catch fish and birds, how to purify water, and other ways to survive in a seaside environment, we walked to a beautiful government-controlled beach and got started.

Well, okay, we hung out on the beach all day!

But it was more than that. We played along with the intent of the class, which at this point was mostly about foraging for food. We caught a few small crabs and other creatures, a meager take. Then, late in the afternoon, several of us started a conversation with some fishermen in a small boat near the shore. As they shouted back and forth, the fishermen drifted closer, and their boat snagged on the line connecting a lobster trap to its float. To untangle themselves they pulled up the trap. It was loaded with lobsters! "These are out of season," they yelled, and started to pour out the precious food sources. "We'll take them!" we hollered. Hey, we were in survival mode.

The resulting seafood stew looked ugly, but it tasted great. And sure enough, we survived.

We slept on the beach under Mylar survival blankets. It was July in San Diego, and SERE School was off to a good start, but I soon learned this was a picnic compared to the rest of the week.

Monday morning we boarded a bus for the two-hour drive to a Navy "camp" in the California desert near Warner

During Navy ROTC summer training we experienced the various career fields that would be available after graduation, which helped some students to decide their direction. This was me during "Marine Corps week." I was already certain I wanted to go fighters, but these experiences were educational.

Timed runs on an obstacle course were a good test of overall physical fitness. I shot this photo during Navy ROTC summer training, before flight school, but we had similar trials in Pensacola.

Standing in front of the T-2 Buckeye basic jet trainer, early in my training. You can see i was a compact design.

The squadron logo for Training Squadron 10—known as "TRARON 10" or just VT-10—in 1979. The squadron nickname was Cosmic Cats. The logo has since been changed and the squadron is now called Wildcats. VT-10 provides basic flight training for future Naval Flight Officers who will crew a variety of aircraft.

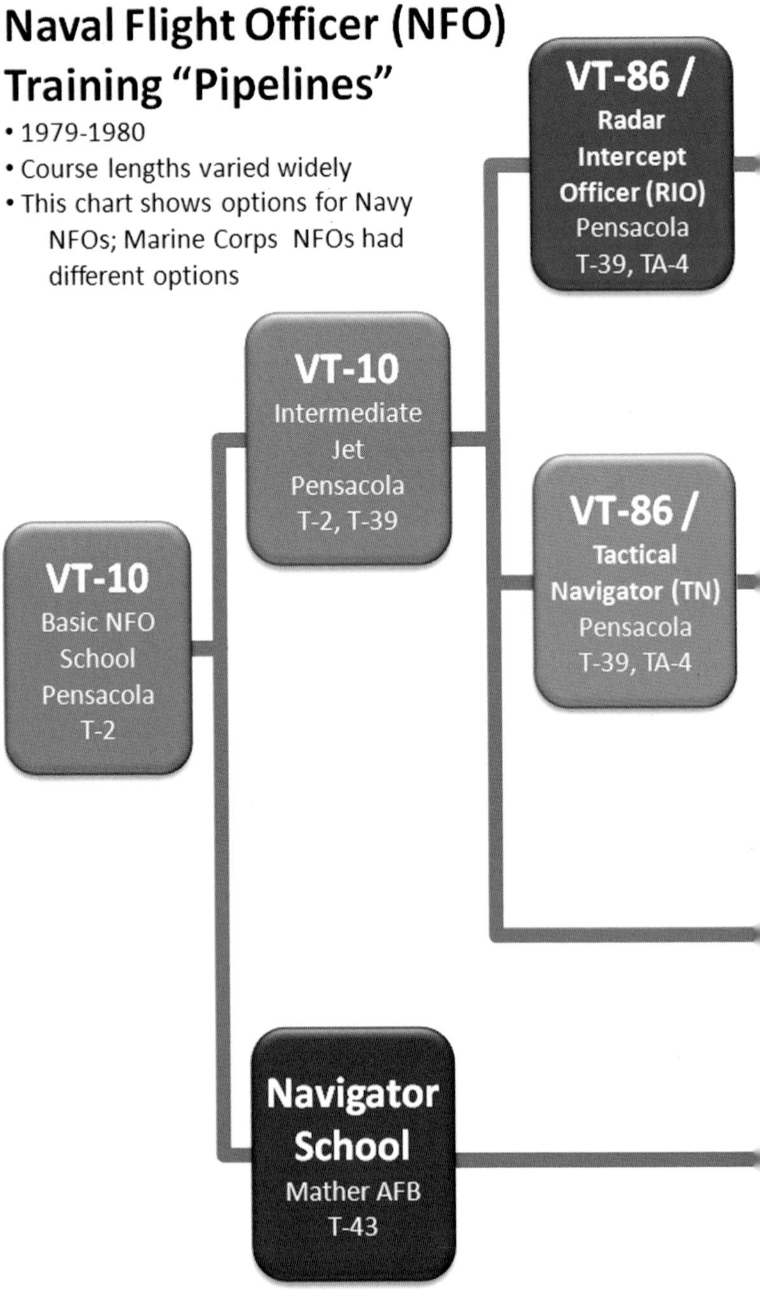


This chart shows the training options for Naval Flight Officers (NFOs) in 1980. Each track was known as a pipeline, and led to the aircraft on the right. The Navy could put Student NFOs into any pipeline, but I only wanted one: the pipeline leading to the F-14 Tomcat.

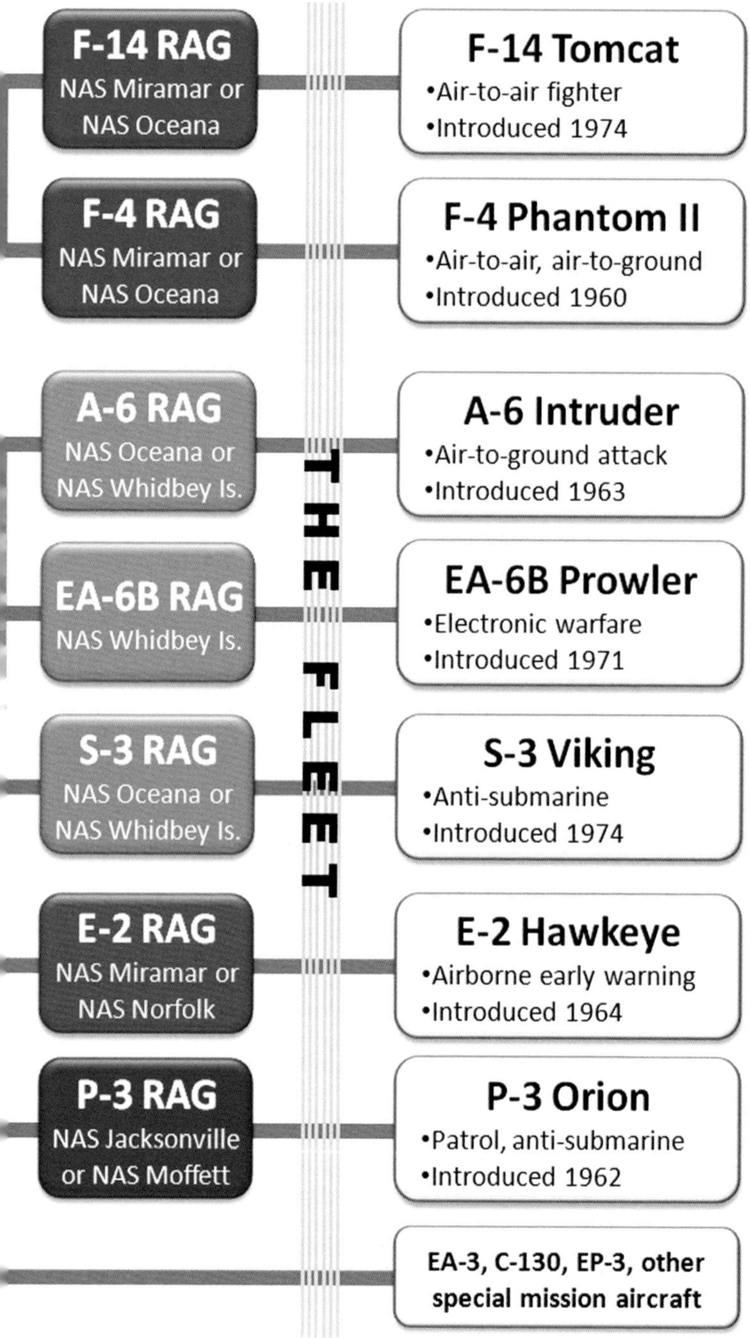
F-14 RAG
NAS Miramar or NAS Oceana
F-4 RAG
NAS Miramar or NAS Oceana
A-6 RAG
NAS Oceana or NAS Whidbey Is.
EA-6B RAG
NAS Whidbey Is.
S-3 RAG
NAS Oceana or NAS Whidbey Is.
E-2 RAG
NAS Miramar or NAS Norfolk
P-3 RAG
NAS Jacksonville or NAS Moffett
THE FLEET
F-14 Tomcat
•Air-to-air fighter
•Introduced 1974
F-4 Phantom II
•Air-to-air, air-to-ground
•Introduced 1960
A-6 Intruder
•Air-to-ground attack
•Introduced 1963
EA-6B Prowler
•Electronic warfare
•Introduced 1971
S-3 Viking
•Anti-submarine
•Introduced 1974
E-2 Hawkeye
•Airborne early warning
•Introduced 1964
P-3 Orion
•Patrol, anti-submarine
•Introduced 1962
EA-3, C-130, EP-3, other special mission aircraft

Enjoying the brilliant white sands of Pensacola Beach. This was a great place to unwind socialize, and even study.

My "ensign-mobile," a 1972 Mustang convertible. It fit my budget and got me around fc a few years.

Flying a T-2 like the aircraft I was in, our wingman joins up in tight formation during a training flight in VT-10. The T-2 was sometimes called "Tubby," for reasons obvious in this picture.

Our wingman in loose formation above dramatic clouds in the afternoon sun.

AVIATION TRAINING FORM INSTRUMENT NAVIGATION, B–5 (T–2)

CNATRA Form 1542/6H5 (REV. 5–79)

SQUADRON (VT) VT–10

**PERFORMANCE APPRAISAL**

| U | BA | A | AA | I/D | | ITEM | COMMENTS |
|---|---|---|---|---|---|---|---|
| | | X | | R | 1 | Preflight Procedures Review (M) | |
| | | X | | P | 2 | Head work | #9 Very Good Pilot Comm |
| | | X | | C | 3 | Aircraft Limits (G7, J7) | 1000' TO COS G/S ✓ 29.92 ETC. |
| | | X | | C | 4 | Emergency Procedures (G8) | |
| | | X | | C | 5 | Jet Log (E4) | |
| | | X | | C | 6 | DD–175 (E5) | #20 Very Good Enroute Course |
| | | X | | C | 7 | DD–175–1 (E7) | |
| | | X | | C | 8 | VIDS/MAFs (Pre/Postflight) (F2) | Control on Course or Corr. |
| | | | X | C | (9) | Pilot Communication (K3) | |
| | | X | | C | 10 | NAVAID Operation (J2) | All the way |
| | | X | | C | 11 | Instrument Usage/Scan (J6, J7, J8) | |
| | | X | | C | 12 | Ground Checklist (G9) | #25 Good Pt. Pts Zig-Zagged |
| | | X | | C | 13 | Departure Communication (K1) | |
| | | X | | C | 14 | Departure/En Route Checklist (G9) | A little more than necessary |
| | | X | | C | 15 | Departure Arcing (H7) | |
| | | X | | C | 16 | Departure Course Control (H7) | #27 Good Holding—Should |
| | | X | | C | 17 | Fuel Transfer Control (J5) | |
| | | X | | C | 18 | Altitude Selection/Compliance (H9) | Have slowed to holding |
| | | X | | C | 19 | En Route Communication (K1) | |
| | | | X | C | (20) | En Route Course Control (H7) | Speed a little sooner |
| | | X | | C | 21 | Turn Point Procedures (Format) (H5) | |
| | | X | | C | 22 | Time Estimates (I1) | |
| | | X | | C | 23 | Fuel Estimates (I1, I2) | |
| | | X | | C | 24 | Inflight METRO Evaluation (I3) | Gen: Good Stud No |
| | | X | | C | (25) | Point–to–Point (H8) | |
| | | X | | C | 26 | Approach Checklist (G9) | Problems. |
| | | X | | C | (27) | Holding (H10) | |
| | | X | | C | 28 | Approach Arcing (H6) | |
| | | X | | C | 29 | Approach Course Control (H7) | |
| | | X | | C | 30 | Approach Communication (K1) | |
| | | X | | C | 31 | Aircraft Pre/Postflight (F1) | |
| | | X | | C | 32 | Yellow Sheets (Pre/Postflight) (F3) | |

| U | BA | A | AA | | ITEM |
|---|---|---|---|---|---|
| | 0 | 30 | 2 | | TOTAL MARKS THIS FLIGHT |
| | 9 | 83 | 12 | 136 | TOTAL CARRIED FORWARD |
| | 9 | 113 | 14 | | CUMULATIVE FLIGHT TOTAL |

AIRSICKNESS (NO)

| | | | |
|---|---|---|---|
| X | UP | | DOWN |
| X | COMPLETE | | INCOMPLETE |
| | WARM UP | | EXTRA TIME |
| | CHECK/SPEC CK/RE CK | | CORRECTION |

| FLIGHT TIME: FT.DUR | SP CR | NITE | ACT INST | APPROACHES: TAC | PAR | ASR | ILS/ADF /VOR |
|---|---|---|---|---|---|---|---|
| 1.3 | 1.3 | 0 | 0 | 1 | – | – | – |

| EVENT | | INSTRUCTOR | RATE | SSN | SIGNATURE |
|---|---|---|---|---|---|
| B–5 | | DAVIS T. | LT | | ~~JACKET REVIEW REQUIRED~~ |
| **ACFT** | **CLASS NO.** | **STUDENT** | **RATE** | **SSN** | **CALENDAR DATE** |
| T–2 | 792Ø | BARANEK, D. | ENS | | 4 DEC 79 |

3.04

BASIC

The gradesheet for one of my early training flights shows how many performance items were graded. I selected this one as an example because I got two above average grades and none below average, and I did not get airsick – which was evaluated every flight.

T-39 Sabreliner trainers wait in the morning fog for a day of training flying in Pensacola.

The small radar scope in the T-39. The radars came from recently-retired Navy fighters, and these basic scopes forced students to interpret symbols and perform real-time calculations to successfully complete an intercept. It was three inches wide and six inches high.

Here I am in the back of the T-39, between runs. In other jets we wore helmets and oxygen masks, but this headgear was appropriate for the cabin of the T-39, which was designed as a business jet.

The sporty TA-4 Skyhawk, cruising above the azure waters of the Gulf of Mexico south of Pensacola.

Dramatic clouds provided a backdrop for many training flights.

As graduation approached, my friend Gary and I went out and took some photos with the white and orange training jets we would soon leave behind. I'm holding my kneeboard in my left hand, and that is the VT-86 squadron logo on the side of the aircraft.

Graduation from VT-86! My mom attended and pinned on my Wings of Gold. Many classmates had family members or significant others in attendance, as it was a milestone on our paths to our dreams. On the left, presenting my certificate, was Commander Robert Flynn, a former A-6 Intruder NFO who was shot down early in the Vietnam War and imprisoned in China for more than five years. Google "Robert J. Flynn."
CREDIT: US Navy photo

Commander Flynn (far left) with our class of newly-minted Navy and Marine Corps NFOs. You can see the wings on our chests. I'm in the back row, just right of center. To the right is my buddy Paul.
CREDIT: US Navy photo

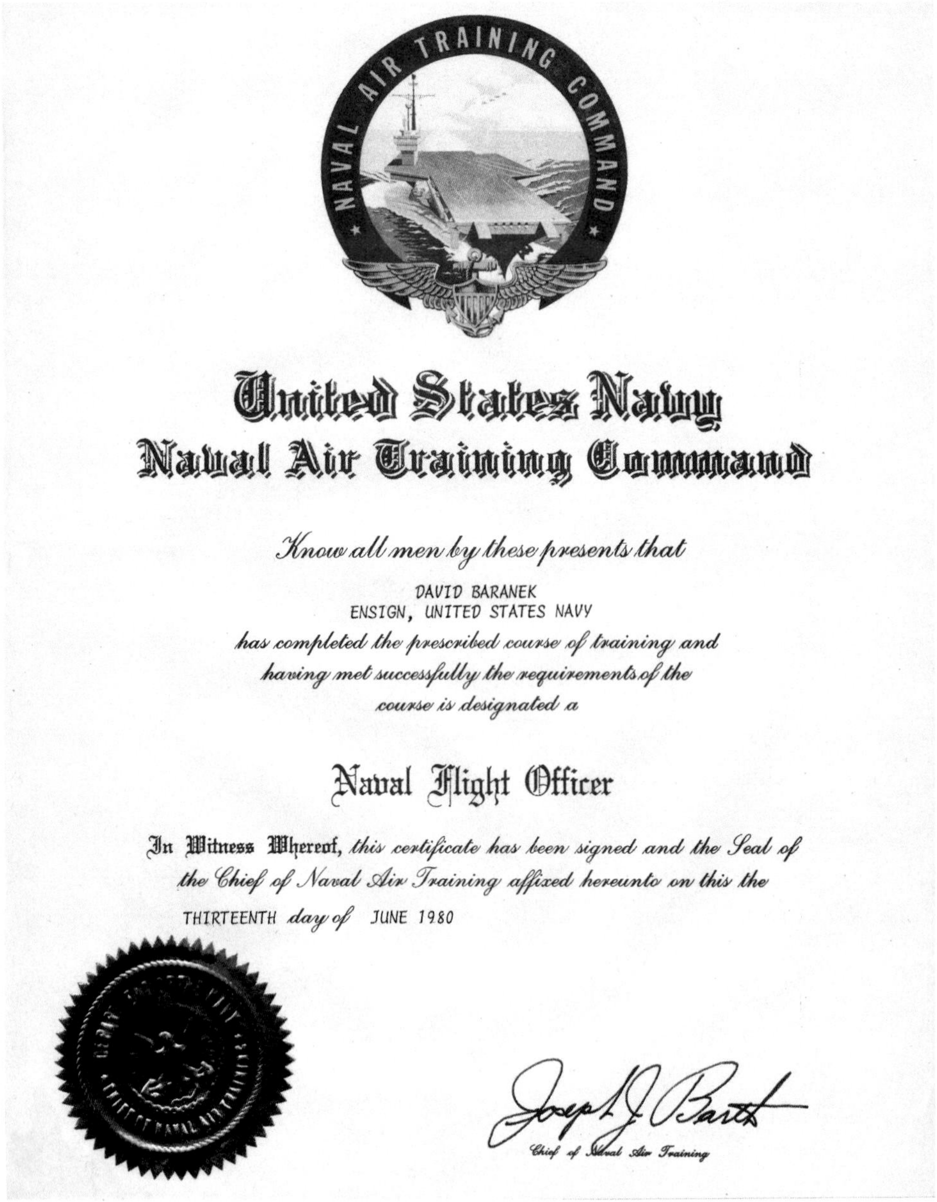

NAVAL AIR TRAINING COMMAND

United States Navy
Naval Air Training Command

*Know all men by these presents that*

DAVID BARANEK
ENSIGN, UNITED STATES NAVY
*has completed the prescribed course of training and having met successfully the requirements of the course is designated a*

Naval Flight Officer

In Witness Whereof, *this certificate has been signed and the Seal of the Chief of Naval Air Training affixed hereunto on this the* THIRTEENTH *day of* JUNE 1980

*Joseph J. Barth*
*Chief of Naval Air Training*

The certificate I received upon graduation, designating me as a Naval Flight Officer.

More important to us than our certificates were the wings we received when we graduated. NFO wings (lower) compared to Naval Aviator (pilot) wings.
CREDIT: Photo by Yves Le Clair via Cédric Bernard

My log book. We were issued logbooks upon arrival in Pensacola, and a squadron yeoman recorded every flight: date, aircraft type and serial number, mission, duration, pilot, and more. This is a recent photo, showing how my "log book" became three books taped together to record nearly twenty years of Navy flying.

An F-14 Tomcat fighter belonging to Fighter Squadron 124 (VF-124), the West Coast F-14 training squadron, cruises above the southwestern United States during my second training flight, a weekend trip from San Diego to Denver.

Our wingman tucks into close formation above the high plains near Denver as we zoom at low altitude near our destination.

Me, Gary, and Ray at Gary's wedding in Houston. Out of college, starting on our chosen careers, we celebrated at every opportunity.

The leather jacket that aviators value so much. This photo was taken early in my days at the RAG and shows patches I had sewn on in Pensacola. *What was I thinking?* I earned the Army parachute wings at "jump school" in Fort Benning while in Navy ROTC, but they were soon removed and replaced by an F-14 squadron patch.

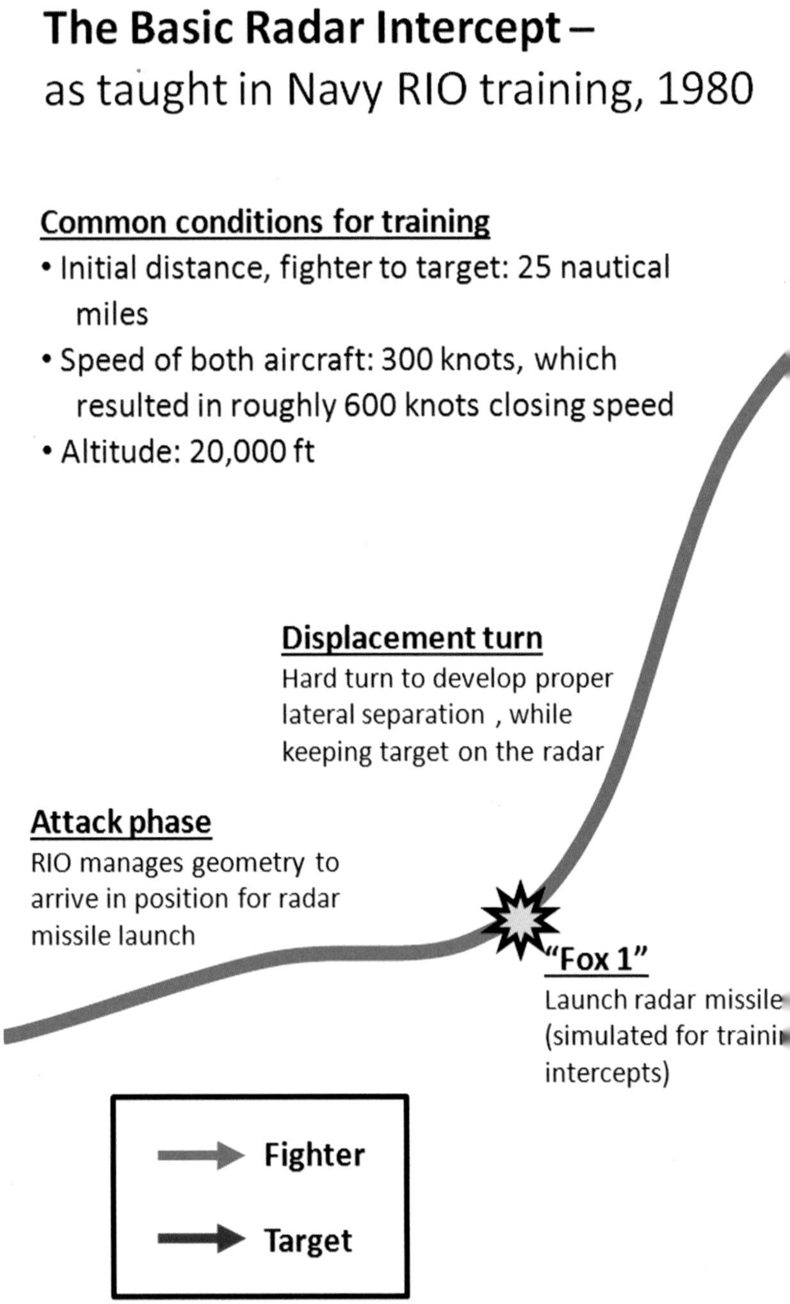


The leather jacket that aviators value so much. This photo was taken earl in my days at the RAG and shows patches I had sewn on in Pensacola. *Wha was I thinking*? I earned the Army parachute wings at "jump school" in For Benning while in Navy ROTC, but they were soon removed and replaced b an F-14 squadron patch.

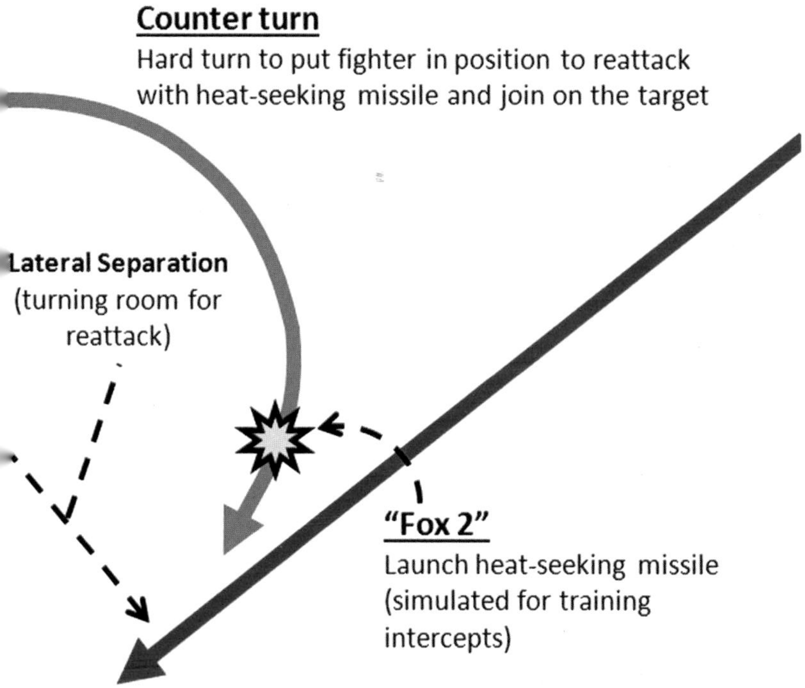


**Complications presented as training progressed**

- Significant altitude difference between fighter and target
- Significant speed difference
- Maneuvers by the target
- Radar degrades for the fighter

Plane captains are junior members of virtually every Navy aircraft squadron, responsibl
for the "care and feeding" of the aircraft. These PCs (the abbreviation for their title) wer
captured on the flight deck of a carrier while washing aircraft.

The patch for VF-124. The symbolism of an F-14 bashing through a book and lamp (knowledge) reflects the squadron's mission as a training squadron. The squadron's official nickname was Gunfighters, but this log prompted some to call them "Bookbusters." Later the patc was changed to resemble the Tomcat patch, which is show later.

Rear cockpit of the F-14 Tomcat. The small screen at the top was raw radar, flanked by controls for the various radar modes and adjustments. The larger screen showed symbology based on radar targets and information such as navigation points the RIO could enter. The hand control at the bottom controlled only the radar antenna, not the aircraft. This was the state of the art when the first Fleet F-14 squadrons became operational in 1974.
CREDIT: Photo by Dave "Hey Joe" Parsons

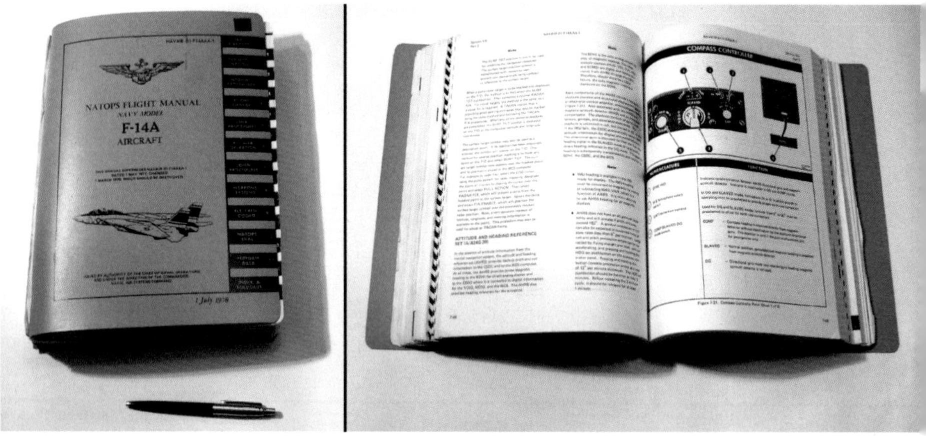


The F-14 NATOPS Flight Manual, the comprehensive source of information and procedures for the F-14. It was sometimes called the "big blue sleeping pill" because of its distinctive cover and the dense technical nature of the text. Pilots and RIOs were expected to know its contents and follow its procedures. Size was roughly 8" x 11", and two inches thick.

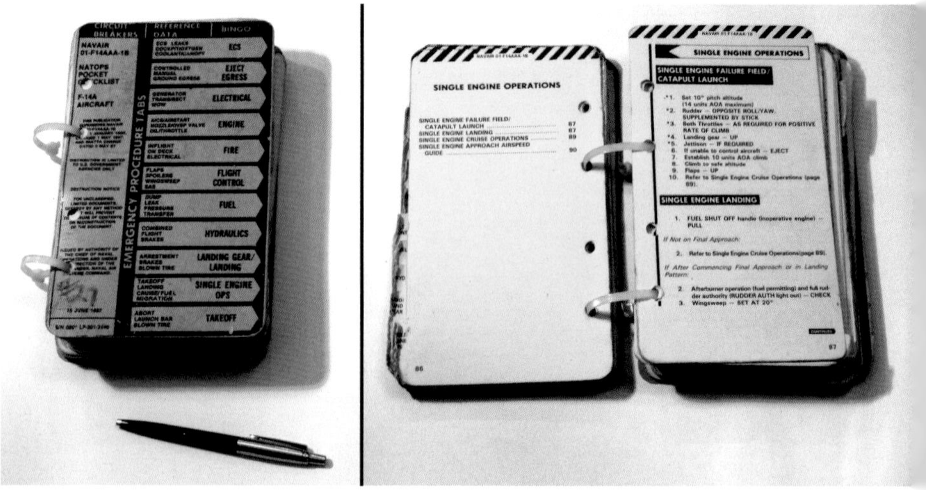


The F-14 Pocket Checklist, or PCL, was the portable version of the flight manual that we carried in the cockpit. It held the "boldface" emergency procedures as well as other information that could be useful in flight. At 5" x 8" and one inch thick, the basic PCL would fit in a pocket of a flight suit or g-suit.

An F-14 flies over the aircraft carrier *USS Nimitz* moments before descending for landing. The carrier is turning into the wind, which reduces the relative speed between the aircraft and the ship and reduces stress on all components.

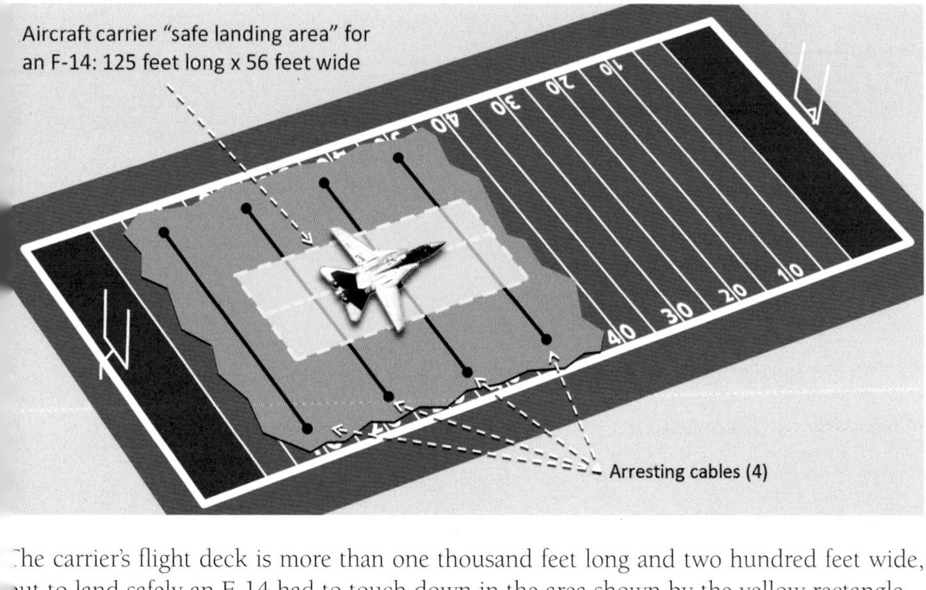


The carrier's flight deck is more than one thousand feet long and two hundred feet wide, but to land safely an F-14 had to touch down in the area shown by the yellow rectangle here compared to a football field for scale. Remember, this was bobbing through the sea at 20-30 mph, often at night. The fact that these demanding operations are “routine” is a testament to the skill of all involved, especially the pilot.

A VF-124 squadron F-14 clears the landing area shortly after an arrested landing. Com
plete attention and close coordination were required of the aircrew and personnel on the
deck. You can get a sense of the F-14's size in this photo.
CREDIT: Photo by Keith Svendsen via David F. Brown

At an altitude of 41,000 feet, an F-14 creates a prismatic halo as it flies in front of the sur
Amazing sights are the aviator's constant companion.

'owerful and sleek, a Tomcat with afterburners ablaze tops billowing clouds. In this photo, treaks of glare on my canopy seem to highlight the fighter's speed.

elfie at 200 mph. My early carrier landings and catapult shots challenged my senses, but ıter I was comfortable enough to take photos. This shot was taken a few seconds after atapult launch, as we banked, climbed, and accelerated to begin our mission.

View from the rear cockpit of an F-14, over the pilot's left shoulder during a tranqu
evening flight.

Afterburner blowout! A split second before the catapult fired, the left afterburner of this F-14 failed, as indicated by the billowy yellow flame instead of a steady blue plume. The jet now has less power than normal. Some deck crewmen have raised their arms in a signal to stop the launch but it was too late, the button had been pushed and the sequence could not be interrupted.

The pilot, Lieutenant Willis "Reefer" Rief, spotted the problem during a final check of his instruments and applied appropriate controls as the jet took to the sky. If the situation wasn't handled correctly, the uneven power from the engines could result in a crash. In one of the "Fleet vignettes" in the book Streak and I lose an engine, but we were at five thousand feet.

For realistic air combat maneuvering training, or "dogfighting," F-14s faced small, nimble aircraft such as the F-5E Tiger II shown here. While the F-5 could not match the F-14 in overall performance it replicated important threat aircraft in the early 1980s and challenged Tomcat aircrews where they needed it most.

During a hard turn shortly after takeoff, our wingman closes in to get into tight formation. We were flying sideways; thinking and operating in three dimensions was a requiremen
to be in fighters.

:arrying two AIM-7 Sparrow missiles and two AIM-9 Sidewinder missiles, my jet waits on he flight line at Miramar before the missile firing exercise (*missilex*) described in one of the 'leet vignettes in this book.

·or the missilex described in the book, our target was an AQM-37 drone like the white ehicle in this photo. The red vehicle is another type of target, and the aircraft behind them · a C-130 that could be used to carry targets aloft before launching them.
REDIT: US Navy photo

Missile launch! I shot this photo an instant after the launch of an AIM-9 Sidewinder. At jus
under ten feet long and 200 pounds, the Sidewinder was smaller than the Sparrow missile
It was used for targets at shorter ranges, although there is overlap in their capabilities.

Air-to-air missiles launch like lightning, with powerful rocket motors boosting them t
speed in a fraction of a second. This is a view from my cockpit of an AIM-9 Sidewinde
launch. I shot this a few years after joining my first Fleet squadron, VF-24. It indicates ho
comfortable I'd become during these demanding events.

hortly after completing the RAG and joining my Fleet squadron, I leaned on an AIM-7 parrow missile for a photo. The moustache eventually came in nicely.

The patch worn by F-14 Tomcat aircrews shows a cat with two tails, echoing a design feature of the aircraft. The cat is also wearing a six-shooter, a reference to the built-in cannon carried by the aircraft.

An F-14 is silhouetted by the afternoon sun aboard an aircraft carrier at sea. The plane captain makes final preparations and the pilot climbs into the cockpit before launching on another flight.

Springs. This was high desert, with sandy ground and a lot of low-growing vegetation, cactus, and prickly pears. It was hot in the daytime and cold at night. The first three days consisted of short classes in the morning, land navigation for the rest of the day, and then practical exercises such as building small shelters. It was similar to the survival course in Pensacola, including the part about being hungry and talking about food. I ate various plants, and yes, a lot of ants, which are not very filling. When I got enough of them in my mouth to actually discern a taste, it was vaguely citrus. Ants were not unpleasant and I ate a lot of them, always being sure to crush the head first to prevent the ant administering what would probably be an unpleasant bite. I slept on the hard ground under my survival blanket and woke up freezing.

Things changed after the Wednesday morning class. We had a short navigation exercise, only this time we had to avoid "enemy soldiers" played by trained Navy personnel. Like most of my fellow SERE-schoolers I successfully avoided the enemy during the navigation segment. This provided little comfort because soon a bell clanged and we all had to report to a collection point. We'd been warned not to remain in hiding after the bell was rung, to avoid what came next in the curriculum. What you would get instead would be even worse.

I was piled into the back of a pickup truck and taken to an "enemy compound" where our class was collected. I spent most of the next hour on hot sand, in the "up" position of a push-up, with the rest of the class. When anyone tried to look around, a guard with a bad accent yelled, "*Keep your eyes on the ground, American pig!*" We heard a lot of yelling and people being thrown around. We were separated into small groups and processed as POWs. I became "war criminal number five-four."

The enemy compound was a large sandy clearing in the scrub, with a guard tower and several simple cinder block buildings. One side was formed by a row of wooden boxes that looked like doghouses. Barbed wire surrounded the compound and structures.

After processing, we were shown to our accommodations: the boxes. Each was about thirty-six inches high, twenty-eight inches wide, and twenty-eight inches deep, which is a tight fit for a person sitting with their legs crossed. Each box had a heavy dark cloth across the front.

During the afternoon, over the long night, and into the next morning we received a small taste of mental and physical duress. We knew that we were US Navy officers being dealt with by other US Navy personnel, but still the exposure was effective. We were kept separated in the small boxes, sometimes blindfolded, not allowed to sleep, punished if we were caught communicating, subjected to interrogations, thrown around, slapped. Many of us experienced another level of training when we were strapped to a "waterboard."

We had heard about the waterboard in the run-up to SERE school. I thought that since I had grown up swimming I would be able to handle it. When it was my turn, I was strapped to a backboard, and I felt only a little apprehension. After all, this was a training environment. In keeping with the code of SERE school graduates, I won't go into detail, but I will say that for the rest of my life I will remember the words, "*Take away his breath, comrade!*"

I am supremely thankful that after leaving Warner Springs, California, I never experienced the waterboard again.

The "POW camp experience" lasted less than twenty-four hours, but we talked about SERE School for weeks.

TEN

# "Here We Go!"

SERE School was an unforgettable experience, but what came next eclipsed it: my first flight in an F-14 Tomcat. It was on a Friday, September 19, 1980, about two months after I started the RAG and less than eighteen months after graduating from Georgia Tech.

Leading up to this, my class's training was progressing as planned, so we knew our first Tomcat flights were coming soon. I had one or two graded simulator runs every day for a week, plus a few lectures. On Wednesday, I got the word that instructor pilot LT Ron Gollhofer was looking for a student to fly a cross-country to Denver with him over the weekend. LT Gollhofer was a Denver Broncos fan, and his callsign was "Crush." By now it was easier for us students to call the instructors by callsigns. Soon we would have our own.

I told Crush I was interested, but before I could go I had to complete my first flight, and squadron rules said it had to be a local flight from Miramar. So on Friday morning at 8:00 I had a simulator that focused on radar use, then at 10:45 I had my "safe-for-flight" simulator. This one covered all standard procedures for a normal flight, plus some emergency procedures. I passed, and was cleared to fly the Tomcat as a Student RIO. The flight brief started at 2:00 on Friday afternoon.

Having completed about forty flights in VT-10 and VT-86, and dozens of Tomcat simulator sessions, I was well prepared—but still excited. The instructor's demeanor, the ready room ambience, the briefing notebook, and all the peripherals were familiar to me from Pensacola. But instead of the background buzz of a weekday morning, this was a beautiful Friday afternoon in San Diego. People were leaving the squadron headed for home or the Officers' Club—as regulars we now called it the O-Club. Things were quiet by the time we finished the flight brief about thirty minutes later and went downstairs to put on our flight gear.

By now it was taking me only a few minutes to get dressed in the g-suit, parachute harness, and survival equipment. For the F-14 we added a new item: leg restraints. These were two thick nylon straps fastened around each lower leg, with a metal buckle at each heel. They connected to the ejection seat and prevented the pilot's and RIO's legs from flailing in the violent windblast in case of a high-speed ejection. Like the shoulder belt of a car, the mechanism allowed free movement of our legs, but in an ejection it would pull them in tight to reduce injury. By now I'm thinking, "Want me to wear more gear? No problem."

Besides, leg restraints looked cool. They said, *I fly fighters.*

I was then initiated into something all Tomcat aviators have experienced: waiting for a jet. By Friday afternoon the Tomcats in VF-124's fleet were running rough after another demanding week of training flights. At RAG squadrons, the pace was unrelenting but the squadron was a lower priority than Fleet squadrons for parts and supplies. The personnel in the Maintenance department worked hard keeping the jets ready to fly. No one would have blamed us if we had just canceled, but I wanted my first flight, Crush wanted to go to Denver, and my first flight was a prerequisite. So we told Maintenance Control that if they could get a flyable jet, we would take it.

The Training department was happy because it would be one more block checked for the week. I'm sure the SDO would rather have called it a day, but Crush said, "Stick around, we're going flying," so the SDO had to stay behind the duty desk. The only limiting factor was sunset. First flights had to be conducted entirely in daylight, even for student RIOs flying with experienced pilots, so we couldn't wait too long. Maintenance finally came up with a jet, and as the plane captain got it ready to fly, we walked out to the flight line in the late afternoon sun.

Nearly thirty Tomcats were parked in three rows on the VF-124 flight line, and scores of other aircraft were lined up on the jet-fuel-stained concrete in mind-boggling numbers. A quarter mile to the west of us, across an unbroken plain of concrete, E-2 Hawkeyes filled squadron flight lines. To the east, the concrete plain extended nearly a mile and was dense with Tomcats and Phantoms. The line farthest east was adorned with Topgun A-4 and F-5 adversary jets. The airfield was uncharacteristically quiet. We were apparently the only people going flying on this Friday afternoon. I concentrated on finding my jet among those on VF-124's line and tried to stay calm while chatting with Crush. I had a lot on my mind.

Crush shepherded me through my first Tomcat preflight that really mattered. He wanted to complete the event, but it wasn't a free pass for me, it was a training session. He quizzed me on the correct readings for the hydraulic reservoir pressure gauges (1,800 psi) and watched me inspect an engine compartment while the PC held open the access panel. We climbed up to the top of the jet to complete the preflight, finishing by inspecting the canopy and ejection seats. Then we pulled the safety pins on our seats and stepped down into our cockpits. The jet was ready and so was I, so we strapped in.

I clipped my leg restraints to the bottom of the ejection seat. The PC stood on the foldout step and helped me strap in and connect myself to the aircraft—oxygen, communications, g-suit. He then helped Crush and backed down the ladder, closing all panels as he went, finally folding the ladder back into its compartment. The PC didn't have to pull the final pin for the F-14 ejection seat, as they did on the T-2, due to the seat's design. It felt like another reminder that I was in the real world now and more responsible for my own safety. I swept through my cockpit switches from left to right as I had done in the training squadrons and Tomcat simulators, while Crush did the same up front. The F-14's rear cockpit had many more switches than the T-2 and TA-4, but with an orderly sweep I was able to complete the setup.

Crush signaled the PC to apply electrical power, which allowed me to use the radio. I put our clearance on request, sounding a little better than I did ten months earlier in VT-10, but I had reverted to using a detailed script until I got used to the new aircraft and airfield. Crush then gave the PC the signal to turn on the high-pressure air supplied through a thick hose, which allowed him to start the engines. They provided air conditioning to all aircraft systems and the cockpit, so I could close the huge Plexiglas canopy.

Over the ICS I said, "Canopy coming."

When Crush said, "Clear," I slid the handle forward with my right hand, and the heavy canopy slowly settled onto the fuselage and slid forward into its locks. I switched the AWG-9 radar and weapons control system onto Standby. I entered our latitude and longitude into the inertial navigation system and turned my attention to the nine-inch tactical information display (TID) screen low in front of me, where I could watch the progress of the navigation system alignment. In the middle of the screen the onboard checkout routine displayed its progress as it ran through checks of electronic systems.

Start-up went smoothly, and I got our taxi clearance from Miramar Ground Control. We taxied past the other Tomcats crouching on silent haunches on the VF-124 flight line. Crush asked how I was doing and I said, "Pretty good, except I can't see any symbols on the TID, just dots." Crush asked if I had pushed all of the display buttons for the TID. "Oh," I said, "that would probably help." That was a colossal understatement. I pushed them and the TID showed the symbols I expected.

I never again forgot to push these buttons on startup, and was proud of myself for not letting this small oversight become a real problem. Crush thought it was good that I didn't get rattled and handled the problem with humor. We taxied to the hold-short area at the end of the runways.

I called for takeoff just before 6:00 p.m., an hour before sunset. With no other airplanes active on the field, Miramar Tower cleared us immediately. We taxied onto the runway, and Crush lined up on the centerline. He pressed the tops of the rudder pedals to apply the brakes, and moved the two throttles forward to military power. The jet's nose dipped as the thrust of the engines compressed the nosewheel strut. With his right hand on the stick, Crush wiped out the controls, then with his left he shoved the throttles forward to minimum afterburner, Zone 2 in the F-14.

"Ready?"

"Yes!"

"Here we go!"

Crush released the brakes as he pushed the throttles forward to maximum afterburner, Zone 5. The afterburner injects pure fuel into a large metal chamber that extends aft of the basic engine, and ignites it. Most fighters have afterburners. They increase the engine thrust by 50 percent or more, and produce a large, visible flame. In the F-14 the burner tube was 3½ feet in diameter, and the plume of flame was impressive. The downside of using the burner is that fuel consumption goes up ten times or more, but that's one of life's tradeoffs. The F-14's afterburners had five stages or zones, so Zone 5 was max burner.

Military power is the common term for highest power from the basic engine, without burner.

I had learned all of this in classes but had never experienced it before. The word "wow" is inadequate to describe a full burner takeoff in a light Tomcat. These RAG aircraft, without missiles or external tanks, qualified as light. The nose popped up when Crush released the brakes and we accelerated down the runway. I called airspeed as I had before, only quicker.

"Off the peg." Seven seconds later: "Sixty knots." Three more seconds: "One hundred knots." And we weighed almost thirty tons!

A few seconds later, Crush eased the stick back a few inches, and the large horizontal stabilizers deflected. Passing 130 knots, less than fifteen seconds after brake release, the Tomcat nosed up—we say "rotated"—and we were airborne!

Crush immediately pulled up the landing gear handle near his left knee, and eased the stick forward a little to fly down the runway without climbing. At 180 knots he raised the flaps.

In this clean configuration we rapidly accelerated along Miramar's 11,000-foot main runway, 24-Right. I glanced at the jets, hangars, and control tower blurring past outside as Crush pulled the jet into a brief climb to the departure altitude of 2,000 feet and turned to the departure heading. This would take us over less-populated areas as we flew five miles to the coast. By now Crush had pulled the throttles back out of afterburner, otherwise we would have exceeded air traffic control speed restrictions. A Tomcat in full afterburner at low altitude is an incredibly powerful machine, as I would learn in the coming weeks and months of flying.

While trying to appreciate the power and blurring scenery, I managed to switch my radio as required from Miramar Tower to San Diego Departure Control. Crush took care of flying the jet as I tried to do my part. This was my first Tomcat flight, and despite the training I was a little behind the airplane. My brain was trying to process all of the new inputs and sensations in addition to fulfilling my duties as a RIO. In a few more flights I would be pulling my own weight, but on this flight Crush kept us out of trouble.

In no time, it seemed, we were over the Pacific Ocean near San Clemente Island. Inhabited only by goats and small temporary crews of Navy personnel, San Clemente is a twenty-mile-long landmark about fifty miles off the coast of Southern California. It was a priceless visual reference point, even with our inertial navigation system.

The sun seemed to move faster than normal as it descended in the western sky, no doubt hastened by our need for a daytime-only flight. Crush made sure that I performed fundamental tasks such as running an airborne systems check and using the radar to search for airliners flying from Los Angeles International Airport (LAX) eighty miles north—no problem for our AWG-9.

We completed a few loops and turns to give me a small sense of aircraft capabilities. He asked if I wanted to go supersonic and of course I said, "Sure!" So he advanced the throttles to Zone 5 again. I felt a purposeful acceleration, and in a few seconds my airspeed indicator said 1.1 Mach. We were moving faster than the sound of our own engines!

Block checked, no drama—but what a ride.

We slowed down to subsonic speed and Crush called the SDO to check on the official time of sunset. We were about to turn into a pumpkin, so he turned east and I called San Diego Approach Control to start our trip home. We landed at, I'd say, the exact time of sunset. In the aviator's fashion of sometimes stretching the truth, that means we were a little late.

Since the flight had gone smoothly and it was now after 7:00 p.m., we completed a quick debrief and arranged to meet at the hangar at 8:00 a.m. Saturday to fly to Denver. I went back to the bachelor officers' quarters—the BOQ— and told Paul and Steve about the flight. I was the first among us to complete my first flight, so I had the best story for a few days, but soon we would all share the experience.

Our weekend trip was great—what else could be said of an overnight trip from San Diego to Denver in an F-14? A student pilot in my class flew in formation with us. He had an instructor RIO in his backseat and it was a graded flight for him, as it was for me. Over the weekend the two aircraft completed a total of four training events that would normally have required several days of flying from Miramar. On the way up, Crush had me demonstrate as much of the weapons system capabilities as I could. We landed at Buckley Air National Guard Base* just outside of Denver. While in Denver we stayed at his parents' home and went to a Broncos football game. But for me the highlight was our departure Sunday evening.

Our wingman left early; Crush and I stayed a little longer. Family time for him, and my daytime-only restriction was gone. We briefed the flight, filed a flight plan, preflighted the jet, and strapped ourselves in. Even though this would be just my third Tomcat flight, many of these functions were similar to what I had experienced in Pensacola, and soon we were ready to go. Crush told me to request an "unrestricted climb," something new to me that would soon become a

* At the time I visited, Buckley was an Air National Guard Base. It later became an Air Force Base, which is its status in 2016.

familiar term. If cleared, we would not have to conform to the stepped climb profiles that accommodated a wide variety of traffic, from propeller-driven Cessnas to 737s, and instead would be able to use our fighter's power and zoom quickly to altitude.

Although it seemed completely reasonable for a fighter, it was still just a request that would have to be made, and granted or not. But air traffic around Buckley was light at the time, so the request was granted. Buckley Tower cleared us to take off and climb unrestricted to 18,000 feet.

We took the runway. Crush pressed the brakes and ran the engines to military power, and the jet's nose dipped again. He wiped out the controls, throttled up to afterburner, checked the instruments, and asked if I was ready to go. I was, and he released the brakes. The nose popped up and we accelerated quickly. I called airspeeds, we rotated, and Crush raised the landing gear and leveled off to fly down the runway as we accelerated.

In the evening darkness, I was keenly aware of the bright blue-white glow of flame from our engines forty feet behind me. Lights on hangars and buildings streaked by in my peripheral vision. I looked at our rapidly increasing airspeed as we neared the end of the runway, and Crush yanked back on the stick to launch us into a steep nose-high climb.

"Buckley Tower, Navy November Juliet 426, airborne, switching Departure." I tried to sound like I belonged here, but I'm sure the controllers in the tower knew that I was both new and loving it.

Since Buckley is about 5,600 feet above sea level, it took quite a bit less than thirty seconds for us to reach our assigned altitude of 18,000 feet. Crush smoothly leveled off while I rapidly switched through the Departure Control frequency and contacted Denver Center. We were cleared to climb to a higher altitude and start the route back to Miramar.

I was storing all the sensations and images in my long-term memory, and looking forward to a nice flight home, when Crush said, "Okay, get some contacts on the radar."

Oh, yeah, I'm a student. Almost forgot.

I pointed the AWG-9 radar antenna southwest—the direction we were headed—to paint any airliners flying toward Denver. In seconds, several contacts appeared on the TID. Shifting to more of a student mode, I reported a contact to Crush: "Single target, 12 degrees left, 85 miles, 33,000 feet, 850 knots closure." I then used both automatic and manual modes to lock targets, to make the radar antenna physically point precisely at a single target and determine detailed information about it. Using the radar to show multiple targets and locking a single target were techniques I had practiced in the F-14 simulator. I would use them at different times in a tactical situation. While I fleetingly resented the reminder of my student status, it was a price to be paid for flying in a powerful two-seat fighter above the western United States on a beautiful Sunday night. My radar work went well and made the flight go quickly. Our flight to Miramar took 2.0 hours, and my grades were 4 Average, 4 Above Average. Okay, being a student RIO wasn't so bad.

That round-trip to Denver was the end of my flying in September. Three flights in three days, then a couple of weeks of simulators, classes, self-paced training, and tests. In October I had six Tomcat flights, several of which were just "rides" for me while my instructor pilot supervised the student pilot in the other jet who was practicing formation flying. I had eight flights in November, five in December, and three in January 1981. The ground-based classes and simulators continued, and we were expected to use the self-study scripted slide-shows, similar to what we had done in Pensacola. I have to admit that the workload was less demanding than it was in college, which means I had plenty of free time, which I enjoyed. In a few months, while in a Fleet squadron, the Navy would get its money's worth out of me.

Training flights in the Tomcat were fantastic, and time in the simulator was extremely valuable in terms of learning about my aircraft and mission. But there were other times that were almost as memorable, such as the days when the weather was terrible, which was actually rare in San Diego. Instructors and students would arrive at the ready room planning to brief and fly, only to confirm what they suspected from their own observations: the weather was so bad we could not conduct training flights. Many adjourned to VF-124's small snack bar (coffee mess in Navy talk) adjacent to the ready room to pass the time, and soon we had a critical mass of personalities there.

All RAG instructors had made at least one extended deployment on an aircraft carrier, most had more than one, and some had flown combat missions in Vietnam. The war ended just five years before I started at VF-124, so those experiences were still relatively fresh. Their tales of the colorful people, strange restrictions, and various episodes ranged from the comic to the tragic and were incredible to hear. Each story would spawn two or three more. And they didn't have to be tales of combat to be exciting: rules governing flying seemed to be getting more restrictive every year. Hearing about Navy fighter pilots and RIOs enjoying the relative freedom of years past was like visiting a supersonic Wild West.

I was not yet a certified Fleet F-14 RIO yet, but I was getting close. Still, graduation wasn't a certainty. Student pilots and RIOs occasionally failed out of the RAG or decided they just didn't want to fly fighters, now that they knew what it was all about. Fewer people left the program than had left in Pensacola, but it happened. As before, they were transferred to other programs to complete their service commitment. One pilot friend who left the program seemed philosophical: flying fighters just wasn't for him, but at least he had logged dozens of flight hours in the fantastic Tomcat. He became a pilot in another Navy aircraft and probably had a great life.

Gary and other friends from Pensacola had arrived in the weeks after my class started. They followed a few weeks behind my experiences, such as the helicopter pickup from San Diego Bay, SERE school, tougher simulators, first flights, and the rough spots as they learned a new aircraft and the fighter mission. Sometimes, we in the class ahead could offer tips and advice; other times we just commiserated over beers at the O-Club across the street from the BOQ. Very convenient.

We were a fraternity of young men striving to excel at our job. We had worked for it, we enjoyed it, and we were getting very good at it. That was a great fraternity to be in.

ELEVEN

# Dogfights in Afterburner

In February we could look ahead just a few months and see the end of our time in the RAG. I'd been at Miramar since July but it felt like I had just started. The fundamental training was done; now we would be learning tactics. It started with realistic radar intercepts and progressed to maneuvering dogfights that would teach us the basics of using the Tomcat's weapons system as we would in aerial combat. RIOs and pilots had gotten a dose of this in our training squadrons, but those flights were pretty basic. Now we were flying a much more complex aircraft on more realistic missions. Not as challenging as what I would soon fly in the Fleet, but they would be among the most stressing missions I had yet flown.

In the simulators and T-39s in Pensacola we used radars designed in the late 1950s. The radar showed a contact as nothing more than a hyphen, and we had to watch its movement and interpret arcane symbols, such as a circle with a gap to indicate the rate of closure, to calculate the situation and direct our aircraft to intercept. We learned to maneuver into position for launching early air-to-air missiles with limited performance. For me, this took a great deal of concentration and training, but it led to a solid understanding of concepts such as lateral separation, turning room, closure rates, and so on, all of which apply to almost every aspect of aerial combat.

In the F-14 I found myself operating a radar designed in the late 1960s. Yes, it was already more than ten years old, but given delays in aircraft design and production it was state-of-the-art in many ways. The Tomcat's AWG-9 radar could scan a much larger wedge of the sky in front of us and could detect targets at much greater range. Instead of the twenty miles' separation we normally started with in Pensacola, we now routinely started thirty or forty miles apart, and the radar could see aircraft more than 100 miles away. We were like kids with a new bike; we even made a word out of AWG-9. Like the first part of "August," to us it was the "awg 9."

The AWG-9 also had different modes that made it better at detecting targets over land, where we would expect to engage enemy fighters in many combat scenarios. In Pensacola we ran intercepts only over the Gulf of Mexico, which was fine for early training. At Miramar we trained over the Pacific Ocean, but also over ranges in southern California and southwestern Arizona near Yuma. The rough terrain added spurious returns known as "clutter" to the radar scope in certain modes, while other modes eliminated the clutter but had their own shortcomings.*

One welcome improvement was that the AWG-9 showed a digital readout of altitude, speed, heading, and other data about the targets. In the T-39 I had used precious brain cells calculating this information, and now it was being fed to me. Instead of analyzing a small tick-mark on the scope to determine antenna elevation and then calculate target altitude—which was always important information—the AWG-9 told me the target was at an altitude of 24,085 feet, along with its speed, heading, and more information. When we saw this in our early RAG classes, I thought, *This should be easy!*

I quickly found out that having the answers does not solve the problem when the test happens at 600 knots and you have to show your work. "How much lateral separation do we have?" an instructor pilot might ask, to test whether I understood the spatial picture. I had to know the answer anyway, to stay ahead of the evolving intercept. If I simply watched the digital readouts and then reacted, I would have to make unusually large corrections or would miss something entirely. With the Tomcat's power and maneuverability we could make up for many mistakes and still get into a firing position, but RAG instructor pilots knew what good intercepts looked like, and that's what they demanded of student RIOs.

* The next generation of fighter aircraft radars solved both problems and was fielded in the F-15, F-16, F/A-18, and an upgraded version of the F-14. For RIOs like me who flew the A-model Tomcat, F-14A, getting the most out of the AWG-9 took a lot of practice and skill.

Intercept training flights started with a single F-14 intercepting a single target, known as a one-versus-one or 1v1. Depending on the learning objectives, the intercept would either end when we got close to the target (known as *merge plot* because that's what it looked like on a ground-based radar, when the two radar returns merged), or would include engaged maneuvering after the merge.

The engagements were more realistic than the maneuvering we had done in Pensacola, when two white-and-orange TA-4s tangled above the Gulf of Mexico. Air combat maneuvering (ACM) in the RAG was now being done in an F-14 Tomcat with an afterburner. Our opponent could be a wily A-4, another F-14, an agile little F-5 Tiger II flown by Topgun, or something else. I even flew several training flights against the Air Force's new F-15 Eagle, when those squadrons visited Miramar. And I had important aircrew duties during engagements, such as operating radar modes designed to improve our ability to lock on to the target and launch a missile or take a shot with our internal gun.

For these flights we would usually accelerate to 350 or 400 knots at the merge, and our movable wings would automatically sweep back (that's called "variable geometry"). We started engagements with a maximum performance turn, pulling six or six and a half g depending on our fuel load. That would slow us down, and the wings would automatically sweep forward to improve our maneuverability. This distinctive feature of the F-14 was fascinating the first few times I saw it. But I was busy, and the moving wings soon lost their novelty.

Air-to-air combat during the Vietnam War showed the F-14's designers, as they were planning its building, that it had to do better in a dogfight than its predecessor, the F-4 Phantom. The F-4 was surely an effective and versatile fighter for its day, but back then it was expected that missiles would dominate the future of aerial combat. So the F-4 was designed without a built-in gun (on most versions) and relatively poor visibility, both of which became liabilities in actual combat. Lesson learned; the F-14 had an internal gun, and a large cockpit canopy with a 360-degree view.

As we progressed through the syllabus, we would face two targets (1v2), which at first was mind-boggling to this student RIO. Suddenly I not only had to describe range and bearing to the target, and run the intercept, but I also had to look closely at the radar return and describe the formation they were flying. It was definitely possible—and later would become almost second nature—but like everything else that was new, it added a level of stress. For me, the RAG was a time to face new challenges in the fighter mission, but not to master them. Mastery would come only after many months and many repetitions.

Next we progressed to 2v1, where two F-14s intercepted and engaged a single target, often a TA-4 Skyhawk flown by the adversary squadron at Miramar, VF-126. Two against one; sounds like overkill, right? Not so; one of the F-14s was flown by a student pilot, and the other was guided by a student RIO. That evened the odds a little, though there were instructors in the other two seats. Being a student RIO, I always came to the fight with an instructor pilot. The 2v1 was a critical stepping stone for students to learn about being a lead or wingman in a tactical situation.

Eventually I flew the main event: 2v2 intercepts to engagements, the greatest tactical challenge I would face in the RAG. One of these was particularly memorable. Our wingman pilot was my Georgia Tech classmate, Sandy Winnefeld, and his RIO was Willy—Bill Driscoll, the Vietnam MiG ace. My instructor pilot was Jimmy Mac, LT Jim McArthur, who would later become an admiral, and our opponents were a TA-4 Skyhawk and an F-15 Eagle.

As with the Tomcat, the designers of the Eagle applied the hard lessons from aerial combat in Vietnam and took advantage of further advances in engines and aerodynamics. The Air Force jet was lighter, unencumbered by the heavy structure that the Tomcat needed for repeated carrier landings, nor by the Tomcat's heavy radar and other systems that came with the Phoenix missile. With its incredible maneuverability, the Eagle was a challenge for the Tomcat.

We were scheduled on the range near Yuma, flying at 20,000 feet, above rough terrain that would challenge the AWG-9 in automatic modes, and me in manual modes. The sky was leaden with a heavy overcast, rare in the desert Southwest, as we streaked eastward toward our opponents. Both groups—the F-14s and the adversaries—were flying at 350 knots for a closing speed of 700 knots. It was cool to have a college friend and a flying legend on my wing.

Our ground controller reported the initial bearing and range to the "enemy," and as the lead RIO I started to direct our attack while checking my radar display. Soon I spotted a contact right where it should be, about thirty miles southeast of us, and I called this on the radio for our wingman's benefit. Willy replied, "My radar is acting up, Dave, you're going to have to run this one."

I glanced over at their jet, about a mile away on our right. His radar problems meant that our two Tomcats would not have the benefit of this incredibly talented and experienced RIO, but we already knew that radars sometimes failed in the real world. With encouragement and a little coaching from Jimmy Mac, I directed us through the intercept, calling an AIM-7 Sparrow missile shot and then describing the radar picture for the wingman. We got a tally-ho on both adversaries, streaked past them at the merge . . . and the fight was on!

Though it was more maneuverable than the TA-4, the F-15 was also larger and easier to keep track of. Even so, duking it out with a nimble little guy and his big brother was challenging as our two F-14s maneuvered aggressively in a vigorous dogfight. I have to admit that the details are a blur; I don't remember who took shots, who won or lost. After about two minutes the fight ended with "Knock it off" on the radio. Both teams flew back to their starting points to set up for another run, like boxers at the bell.

One thing I do remember: Driscoll's radar was fully functional on the second and third engagements of the flight. Did I get "sandbagged," an old trick of instructors to see how I would handle it? Or did he just have a knack for fixing an AWG-9 during a dogfight? I'll never know, but I do know I was in awe of his radar and communication skills. He definitely lived up to his reputation.

Later, after I completed the RAG and joined my Fleet squadron, I would log a long list of flights in a short span of time. Using the displays and processing the information was like orchestrating a thunderous aerial ballet, and in time it would become almost second nature. But getting to that point was like the violinist asking someone on a street corner how to get to Carnegie Hall. The answer: practice, practice, practice.

I eagerly studied the course material, continued to use my personal-assessment notebook, and kept a good attitude. I did well enough in these flights to meet the requirements. But in my tactical infancy I could not truly appreciate the experience. I was an integral part of the state-of-the-art F-14 Tomcat community, but at this point I was just trying to pass graded events. The challenges would increase in the months ahead, keeping pace with my experience and giving me a deeper appreciation of the fantastic new life I was about to begin.

Radar contact, single-target-track, simulated missile launch. Hard turns to control the spatial relationship between fighter and target. Tally-ho, merge plot, afterburner engagement. Less than two years out of college I was exactly where I wanted to be. High-g turns, displacement roll, guns tracking, simulated kill.

Knock it off. Join up. Repeat.

TWELVE

# Zero to 150 in Two Seconds

In our final months at the RAG my class was scheduled to qualify for aircraft carrier landings. Two syllables are handier than eight, so carrier qualification shrank to CQ, but in aviator slang we just said we were "going to the boat." Since the RAG's mission was to produce combat-ready aircrews, and Tomcats flew combat missions from carriers, we had to meet the Navy's stringent requirements for CQ—written, as we all knew, in blood. The student pilots had already been through carrier quals, flying solo in the T-2 and TA-4 Skyhawk. For them the huge Tomcat, with its incredible number of moving parts and the sheer muscle it took to manhandle its controls, would be even more demanding.

On the other hand, the new student RIOs had never been to the boat.

If I was not in over my head, I was definitely up to my chin.

RAG training managers matched most student pilots up with instructor RIOs, or with seasoned RIOs back for retraining after a staff tour. Student RIOs were paired with more experienced pilots. Our class had only one pair where both guys were new to the Tomcat: my friend Paul was assigned to qualify with a new pilot, Bob Thompson. This showed the confidence our instructors had in their abilities.

My ego would have appreciated a similar vote of confidence, but I was assigned as the RIO for a pilot who had already completed a Fleet squadron tour in F-4 Phantoms, LT Dave "Barnyard" Bernhard. Barnyard was transitioning to the Tomcat to become a RAG instructor. My ego was happy to know that my butt was being taken care of in this dangerous environment.

Preparing for CQ became our priority. We had completed almost all of our intercept and dogfight training flights, and now focused on field carrier landing practice, or FCLPs. Each flight consisted of six to ten touch-and-go landings at the field. But instead of the long runway, we aimed for a small rectangle painted on it. That was the size of the landing area on a carrier. Pilots had to land on it, but they didn't aim for it; they concentrated on the bright light of the optical landing system next to the runway.

The optical landing system is an ingenious device: a vertical row of bright yellow lights with narrowly focused beams, and a horizontal row of green lights as a reference. The pilot will see only one of the yellow lights, and it will be above or below the line of green lights, depending on whether the aircraft is above or below glideslope. If the yellow light is in line with the green lights, the pilot is on glideslope for a safe landing. The yellow light is known as the *meatball*, or just *the ball*.

To start an FCLP session, Barnyard and I would take off from Miramar and fly over the Pacific for fifteen to twenty minutes to burn down fuel to maximum landing weight. This also allowed him some "warm up" time in the jet. We then returned to the base and entered *the break*: flying the length of the runway at 600 feet and 350 knots or more, we made a hard left U-turn to position the plane 1.1 miles away from the runway. This is the fastest way to get back to an airfield, slow to landing speed, and set up for getting the aircraft on deck. Completing the turn, we lowered our gear and got the plane down to our landing speed of 128 to 134 knots (depending on weight) when we were abeam that carrier-size landing area painted on the runway. We would coast for a few seconds more, then roll into another left U-turn at 27 degrees angle of bank, and begin a measured descent. These numbers had been determined when the F-14 was new. When flown properly, the turn would put us on runway centerline at about one mile, where Barnyard would see a centered ball, roll out of the turn to wings level, and fly the final approach.

Here's where it gets interesting. On final, Barnyard must keep up a very disciplined scan of three indicators: the ball, his line-up with the broad centerline stripe on the runway, and the airplane's angle of attack as it approaches stall speed.

Angle of attack has nothing to do with weapons; it's how the wing is "attacking" the air. And "stall" has nothing to do with the engines. Here's what happens. As a wing slices through the air, its shape creates an upward push called "lift" that overcomes gravity and keeps the airplane aloft. But when the wing attacks the air at too steep an angle, the air no longer flows smoothly over it. Instead it flutters and burbles, and the wing loses lift. The control stick shakes, the airplane shudders, and the wing no longer flies. That's a stall. If you're high enough, you can recover by dropping the nose to reduce the angle of attack. But if you're low and slow on final approach, chances are that, as aviators put it, you've bought the farm.

Now you know why Barnyard had to constantly monitor these three items—meatball, line up, and angle of attack while flying the jet near a stall.

While he was working near the limits of the human brain's capacity, I was backing him up by looking over his shoulder to monitor the same scan items. But I added airspeed to my scan. While we were flying the ball, Barnyard wanted to hear only one thing from me: airspeed information. "One knot fast," I would tell him, or "Two knots slow," or "One knot slow." In all my years of experience, most pilots wanted to hear the same thing: How's our airspeed?

Together we hurtled toward the concrete runway, descending at ten feet per second. Barnyard worked the stick and throttles gently and precisely to fly our twenty-six-ton fighter to a touchdown in a rectangle only slightly larger than a basketball court. He was concentration personified, and I was doing all I could to . . . *whomp!* We slam onto the runway in what some call a controlled crash, Barnyard goes to military power, we leap back into the air, turn downwind, and set up for another pass.

When you touch down, roll a bit, and then take off again, that's called "touch and go." FCLPs are more dramatic; they're rightly called "bouncing."

Sound complicated? Sound demanding? Remember, we were training so we could land on a moving aircraft carrier in the middle of the ocean, day or night, under all but the worst weather conditions and possibly after combat operations. Doing this safely would require skill and precision every time. To oversee the entire operation, landing signal officers (LSOs) were stationed beside the runway near the ball, where they carefully observed and graded every single pass.

Landing signal officers are seasoned pilots with special training for this demanding job. It is an additional duty for pilots drawn from all fixed-wing squadrons, and they volunteer for it. In earlier times, the LSO was the carrier pilot's only guide for approach and landing. He stood at the edge of the deck with what looked like a giant Ping-Pong paddle in each hand, waving signals to the pilot on approach and finally giving him the "cut" to hit the deck. Today, even with the "ball" as the pilot's guide, LSOs are on the flight deck to oversee *every* carrier landing. Using shorthand codes and standard terminology, an LSO makes real-time comments on the approach and landing, which are written down by a "writer" and used to debrief the pilot afterward. LSOs make a major contribution to the safe performance that has become the standard for this challenging phase of flight. When RAG LSOs were preparing student pilots for CQ, their role expanded to improving pilot skill as well as ensuring safe landings.

If all this sounds daunting, hold on; there's one more catch. In the real world of carrier ops, the most challenging landings are the ones at sea on dark nights, when all you can see are the ball and centerline lights. At the RAG, if we flew FCLPs at Miramar in the daytime, the terrain provided plenty of visual cues. Made it too easy. The solution? Do most FCLPs at night, *and* do them at remote fields, away from the bright lights of Miramar. To provide the greatest challenge—that is, "the best training"—we flew these night bounces at San Clemente Island, and at the Naval Air Facility outside the small town of El Centro, California, some 100 miles east of Miramar. San Clemente was surrounded by ocean, and El Centro by dark farmland, so both provided precious few references for the pilot to rely on. It was almost like being in the Fleet.

We liked to tell our friends that FCLPs were like "practicing bleeding." But we knew this demanding endeavor was making us ready for routinely doing what is possibly the most challenging thing you can do in an airplane: landing it safely on a rolling, pitching ship speeding through the billows in the open sea at night. Here's how focused my RAG class was on carrier quals: In three weeks, Barnyard and I flew 15 FCLP flights and only three for other training.

I felt I was doing okay with my RIO duties, but I also knew that Barnyard would keep us alive. I made the standard radio transmissions as we approached the landing pattern. I went through the checklists, and gave Barnyard the few advisory calls he wanted: "One slow . . . one slow . . . on speed." But as a new RIO flying with an experienced pilot, for routine approaches and carrier landings I was definitely in a supporting role.* My turn to lead would come as we gave the Tomcat other jobs to do.

* This may seem overly modest, but I am referring to my role as a student RIO, especially with Barnyard in the driver's seat. He was new to the F-14 but an old hand at carrier landings in his F-4 tour. There were times when the RIO was critical to a successful carrier landing—a RAG instructor RIO with a new pilot, for example, or that sudden moment in the Fleet when something would "spook" a pilot. That's rare, but it does happen, and you never know when. But in normal Fleet ops with qualified pilot and RIO, they functioned as a coordinated crew.

Once we completed our FCLP sessions, it was time to carrier qualify. We flew our jets across the country to land on the only carrier available at the time, USS *Nimitz* (CVN-68), which was operating off the coast of Virginia. CQing a dozen students on the opposite coast was a big undertaking. We had to fly six Tomcats from Miramar to Oceana, plus a C-9 cargo jet for the maintenance personnel and essential tools and supplies. Later I would learn that this type of operation was routine for a Navy squadron.

As a student, I had to fly over in the C-9 instead of an F-14. That wasn't all bad; they were essentially airliners, so the flight was relaxing. We flew over on a Thursday, and no events were scheduled for Friday. Saturday night Barnyard and I had a final warm-up session, bouncing at an outlying field near NAS Oceana called Fentress. Although civilization has gotten closer in the decades since, at the time it was pretty dark out there, similar to El Centro. I was still getting used to working on Saturday nights, but we had to, mainly because Fentress was shared by about twenty F-14 and A-6 Intruder squadrons based at Oceana, including the East Coast RAGs, and this was the only time slot available.

I wasn't scheduled on Sunday. On Monday Barnyard and I briefed, manned up, and launched into ugly skies. We were pumped! After an intense month of training we were about to complete our final qual. We knew it would be dangerous, but we chose this job, risks and all.

We were in and out of clouds as we flew east from Oceana, and were surprised to find *Nimitz* operating just a few miles offshore. But the weather for hundreds of miles was terrible, and the best chance for decent weather was the area near the Virginia coast. Even there it wasn't good enough for normal Fleet operations, let alone the unusual nature of RAG CQ. Operations soon bogged down, and after an hour the people in charge decided there was no way we would get our chance that day. They sent us back to Oceana.

We tried again on Tuesday. We briefed mid-morning, manned our jet, and took off with two other VF-124 Tomcats into heavy clouds, the sky only a little better than on Monday. *Nimitz* had moved to fifty miles off the coast, and as we approached we were put into holding patterns at different altitudes—standard procedure for operating in bad weather. I had been flying as a student RIO for more than a year and had logged more than 150 flight hours, so I knew what to do. We orbited alone and listened to the radios as planes were called down from their holding patterns. Occasionally we changed one radio to listen to operations on the flight deck, and it sounded like things were going okay. CQ was always more complicated than regular carrier ops, and required more talking on the radios, but it sounded like this team was working smoothly.

After an hour of waiting we were called down. Our workload changed as we shifted from lazily boring holes in the sky to following the heading and altitude assignments given by *Nimitz* radar controllers. For me, time sped up. Skilled controllers vectored us during our descent through thick layers of clouds and open patches like gray caverns in the sky. Though I had trained for this, I have to admit it was a challenge to keep up the airplane, due to excitement about my first carrier landing. But I was aided by the trusty script on my kneeboard, and descending through an altitude of 5,000 feet I called "Gunfighter 41, Platform" on the radio.

"Platform" was a safety call that confirmed to our controllers that we were aware of our altitude.

Barnyard slowed our descent. Soon we were level at 1,200 feet above the choppy blue-gray seas, cruising at 250 knots. It was comfortable to be below the clouds and flying by visual reference, though of course we still complied with our controller's instructions. This was all standard procedure for bad weather ops. Barnyard was calm; he had probably made 200 carrier landings by this time in his career, though none of them in an F-14. Ten miles out, he grabbed the landing gear handle near his left knee—it was shaped like a miniature wheel on a shaft—and firmly moved it to the "DN" position. We felt the normal rumbling of heavy components being moved by powerful hydraulics. This was my cue to start the landing checklist.

"Ten miles, landing checklist," I said over the ICS. "Wings."

"Wings, twenty degrees, auto," Barnyard confirmed.

"Gear."

"Three down and locked."

We completed the checklist, and I rechecked seven times that the tailhook was down. Okay, that was just in my mind, but Barnyard probably rechecked it at least that many. Our practice landings had been on airfields, with the hook up, and we wanted to get this critical change correct. There would be no danger to our aircraft if we showed up behind the ship with our hook up, and the LSOs would surely notice and call, "Hook down." The danger would be to our wallets, as aircrews who made this mistake were expected to buy at least one round of drinks at the O-Club for everyone in the squadron. Pilot and RIO rightfully shared the cost. We did not make this mistake.

The additional drag from the gear and flaps slowed our jet to landing speed of 134 knots (roughly 150 mph), and Barnyard had to add power to maintain airspeed and altitude. Everything was going smoothly. Suddenly we were only three miles from the carrier and it was time to begin our final descent. Our approach controller called, "441, three miles, begin final descent."

Barnyard reduced power and set up a descent of six hundred feet per minute, the standard for carrier landings. I compared our altitude to our distance from the carrier using a reference card on my kneeboard, and verified that our approach was going as it should. I checked our airspeed and every few seconds reported to Barnyard on the ICS: "On speed. On speed. One fast. Two knots fast. On speed."

To check our rate of descent, I looked over Barnyard's shoulder at the vertical speed indicator on his instrument panel, which was about seven feet in front of me. And, of course, I took a peek at the carrier through the windscreen. My brain was 100 percent occupied with our situation and my crew duties, so I didn't have time to enjoy the view as a passenger, and I didn't have enough experience to process everything as a fully functioning RIO. It took twenty-seven seconds to cover each mile, but things seemed to happen much faster. At two miles our altitude was 860 feet, and at one mile 460 feet.

Though there were heavy clouds above, it was clear near the surface and visibility was excellent. We could see the yellow meatball outside of one mile, and that was reassuring. As we got to one mile from the carrier, I prepared for my speaking role by re-checking our side number, written on my kneeboard (441). Five seconds later, at three-quarters of a mile, I keyed my UHF radio and said, "Gunfighter 441, Tomcat ball, state six-point eight, pilot Bernhard."

The reply from the LSO: "Roger ball, Tomcat. Looking good."

Normal carrier operations were flown in radio silence, but during CQ small comments increased the safety factor, not to mention the pilot's confidence.

We were about fifteen seconds from landing. Barnyard and I fully concentrating on landing our Tomcat. Ahead of us, the personnel on the carrier were focused on safely and efficiently handling the planes that had just landed and bringing our jet aboard. To give a sense of the activity, I asked my friend former F-14 pilot and LSO Paul "Nick" Nickell, to describe the scene on the flight deck:

*What the LSO did not tell Barnyard in his radio reply was that there was a good chance that the F-14 might not get aboard on this approach. As the LSO responded to Bio's "ball call" through a hand held radio transmitter/receiver in his left hand, his right hand held the "pickle" vertically above his head. The pickle was a hand grip with a button for the wave-off lights that could be pressed by his trigger finger, and a button for the cut lights that could be pressed by his thumb.*

*"Foul deck!" yelled the LSO spotter/talker as the corresponding deck status lights flashed red. The F-14 that had landed ahead of Barnyard and Bio had a problem expeditiously clearing the landing area, and this delay now jeopardized their approach. The LSO holding the pickle above his head was a visual reminder that the deck was not ready for the next landing.*

*When Barnyard was only a half mile from touchdown, the arresting gear wire caught by the previous aircraft was starting to retract like a long snake disappearing into holes on each side of the landing area. During their approach, the LSO was monitoring aircraft line up with the help of a small television screen on the LSO platform, showing the view from a camera mounted in the flight deck on the centerline of the landing area. On the screen, crosshairs were displayed. The vertical line was an excellent tool for helping the LSO judge aircraft line up because he was actually standing well left of the landing area. The horizontal line, however, was not very accurate for judging glide slope. For that, the LSO relied on the experience of watching thousands of aircraft carrier landings. The LSO could judge aircraft speed by the attitude of the aircraft; things such as the relationship of the wings with respect to the horizontal stabilizer, and how much of the underside of our aircraft he could see.*

*Barnyard was now at a quarter of a mile. With his right hand still held high above his head, the LSO was starting to massage the wave-off button with his trigger finger. The previously caught arresting cable came taut across the flight deck. It made a few slight oscillations, then stood still. Moments later the LSO spotter/talker bellowed out, "Clear deck, gear/lens set F-14 Tomcat!" as the deck status lights turned green. The LSO dropped his right hand to his side and concentrated on the final segment of the approach. Barnyard and Bio were coming aboard!*

Barnyard's total concentration and expert flying continued, as did my instrument scan and occasional airspeed calls. The carrier steadily increased in size until it filled the windscreen—my perception doubtless affected by my focus on the looming ship. "On speed. On . . ." *OOF!* We thudded onto the flight deck and caught the number three arresting wire. Barnyard jammed the throttles to military power, the standard procedure in case we didn't actually catch a wire, but we quickly decelerated as the powerful arresting gear machinery hauled our 52,000 pound jet from 150 mph to a stop in less than two seconds. The forces and machinery are nothing less than impressive, and the fact that this was a routine operation did not diminish my awe.

My first carrier landing was complete. We called these landings "traps." I have recreated it here, but when I thought about it in the following days, I realized I could remember very few details. Like so many other parts of my flying career, experience would greatly improve my ability to process, evaluate, and appreciate what I was doing and what was going on around me.

But at the time there was no time to pause to mark an early milestone in my career, or Barnyard's transition to a new fighter. Preppy and Rums were right behind us, and another Tomcat was behind them.

People who fly have a favorite joke, but when carrier flyers say it, they're almost serious: It's a good landing if you can walk away from it, and it's a great landing if they can re-use the airplane. This must have been a great landing, because a flight deck director immediately and skillfully guided us in a right turn to clear the landing area, and passed us to the next director. That one signaled a left turn and we headed toward the catapults on the bow. Because we were taxied directly to the catapult and the flight deck was relatively uncrowded, we left our wings out.

Barnyard managed to say, "What do you think of that, Dave?"

All I could say was, "Wow!" My brain was back around the three mile point.

I gave a thumbs-up to a VF-124 flight deck chief to show that the aircraft was good to continue flying. I scanned our wingtips, and saw that we had plenty of room; the directors didn't taxi us near anything. For the first time, I had a cockpit view of the incredible activity on a carrier flight deck, where dozens of sailors scurried around in a complex, well-orchestrated flurry of motion.** They wore different colored jerseys and flotation vests to indicate their job: yellow for those who directed aircraft by hand signals, green for arresting gear and catapult crew, purple for refueling personnel, and other colors for other jobs. Most were eighteen to twenty-one years old, and their higher-rank supervisors were in their mid- to late-twentiess.

The weather for them was pretty good that day: fifty degrees with a steady breeze caused mostly by the carrier's movement, and they weren't getting rained on. They had to contend with roasting-hot jet engine exhaust, the piercing noise of those engines—especially at full power for launch—dangerous jet intakes, moving aircraft, and dozens of other hazards. For protection, they all wore helmets and noise-deadening headsets. It was a typical day for them. Yet they moved quickly and purposefully, getting the job done under these conditions for hours at a time. Sometimes I would see one catching a minute of rest on a pile of hoses or against a steel bulkhead, and I wondered how they could rest amidst all the action!

Once again, former F-14 pilot Nick takes us into the front seat of the Tomcat to give a pilot's view of taxiing on the

** The flight deck crew was predominantly men. There may have been a few women aboard, though their presence would be temporary: at the time of my CQ women could be plane captains in the RAG, and some were probably in the VF-124 support group. But women could not be assigned to units that would participate in combat, such as aircraft carriers or Fleet aircraft squadrons.

flight deck:, a seemingly routine activity in an environment where nothing can be treated as routine:

*While RIOs had the time—and the duty—to observe things going on around the flight deck, about 98 percent of Barnyard's visual scan was on one thing, the taxi director. Several directors were positioned strategically along the route from the landing area to the catapult. Each would direct the aircraft taxiing through his area and then, through hand signals, pass the pilot off to the next director. The speed of their hand movements gave aircrews an indication of whether they were taxiing too fast or too slowly. For full turns they would point in the direction of the turn, while a head or body leaning in one direction meant a slight turn that way. Fortunately these guys were masters because on a busy flight deck, every inch was critical. Barnyard's task was to follow their directions precisely. If he didn't, they would communicate that to him through some very animated body language and hand signals! With a rolling, pitching, slippery flight deck, taxiing could be a real challenge. Sometimes pilots would have to use the brakes to keep the speed down; sometimes they would have to advance the throttles to keep moving forward at all. The other 2 percent of Barnyard's visual scan was used to sneak a quick peek at the engine exhaust nozzle indicator dials above his left knee any time he advanced the throttles. If he advanced the throttles too far forward, more than about a quarter of an inch, the exhaust nozzles would start to reduce in size. This greatly increased the thrust, which helped increase taxi speed; however it dramatically increased the exhaust velocity and the potential of blowing a sailor down or even off of the flight deck.*

Suddenly a sailor ran toward our cockpit and stopped about twenty feet away. He hoisted a box with changeable numbers over his head—the weight board, showing our aircraft weight so I could confirm it. This would be relayed to the catapult crew, to set their machine correctly for our aircraft weight and fuel. I used hand signals to correct the weight, gave him a thumbs-up when it was right, and he scurried off to pass the info to the cat crew.

Barnyard wanted to ensure we did everything correctly. "Let's get the takeoff checklist," he prompted me. I flipped to that page in the reference book clipped to my kneeboard and glanced at it while maintaining my scan outside the jet.

"Brakes," I said, starting the list of mandatory items to check before every takeoff. Though we completed the checklist every flight, it was something I never memorized. I always used an actual printed checklist and carefully kept track of our progress. Missing an item could cause serious difficulty or a mishap, and the dynamic and unforgiving carrier flight deck environment made it more challenging and more important.

"Brakes check okay, accumulator pressure up," Barnyard replied.

Dividing my attention between the checklist and other activities, I continued through the remaining sixteen items as we were directed into place and hooked up to the catapult. That hookup took skill, for both pilot and deck crew. Our jet was 63 feet long, with a 64-foot wingspan, and weighed about 50,000 pounds at this point. The flight deck was rolling, and people and aircraft were buffeted by a steady wind of 20 knots or more. Despite these conditions, the director used hand signals to guide Barnyard into position with an accuracy of inches.

We completed the checklist and were positioned in the cat. Barnyard said, "Ready to go?"

I'm sure my excitement was evident as I replied, "Ready!"

Beneath our plane, sailors ensured we were correctly positioned. We rolled forward a few feet to engage the fitting that would throw us into flight, and I felt a *thunk* as the catapult reeled up the slack to make a solid connection. To our left a shooter raised his hand and gave Barnyard the signal to go to full military power. Barnyard advanced the throttles, checked his engine gauges, and said, "Control wipeout. Forward, left, aft, right."

As he jammed the control stick to its limits to ensure everything was working correctly, I looked at the control surfaces I could see on each wing and the rudders. I said, "Looks good."

Outside, VF-124 personnel were also watching the wipeout and taking a final look for any other problems. Seeing none, they signaled thumbs-up, which the shooter acknowledged. Barnyard had completed every check. He looked at the shooter. He saluted.

The shooter took a last look down the catapult track. Then, with a dramatic sweep of his arm he dropped nearly to one knee and touched the flight deck, as if he were hurling the Tomcat off the deck himself. On this signal, a young sailor in the deck-edge catwalk pushed a button and the catapult fired, sending us on a head-snapping, eyeball-rattling ride down the track from zero to 150 knots in about two seconds. That was my first "cat shot."

"Gunfighter 441, airborne, state 6.2." I made this call as soon as I felt I could speak normally after that launch. As with radio calls during the final approach, regular carrier ops were conducted in radio silence, but during CQ we wanted to ensure various controllers could track the action:

the carrier's air traffic controllers, the squadron that was tracking aircrew qualifications, and others.

"Roger 441. When level at twelve hundred feet, turn downwind and switch button 14." That was the preset radio frequency for our approach controller.

The rest of the flight was a radar-controlled mash-up of a merry-go-round and roller coaster, which actually was a great combination for a new guy like me. Over the next few hours we made five more arrested landings, each followed by a cat shot, and a couple of touch-and-goes to get Barnyard a healthy dose of ball-flying experience in his new fighter. Along the way we were held on the flight deck to refuel, and we spent some more time in a holding pattern while others got their quals. It was an afternoon of dynamic flying and 3.9 hours in the cockpit!

It would have been a remarkable day if it ended there, but it didn't. We returned to Oceana mid-afternoon, got something to eat, then got briefed for the next big event: night carrier qualification.

THIRTEEN

# "You're a Qual."

A simulator does a good job of training you for night flying and landing on a carrier in the dark. You learn to rely on your instruments to get you to final, where you are guided by the pattern of lights on the carrier deck. That is the practical side. Then you do it for real, and suddenly it's a very different story. The simulator was a box on solid ground, but now your inner ear is telling your brain that you're moving, you're leaning, you're bumping over ripples in the air. You do everything you did in that stationary box—everything except shut it off and walk away. Like the background music in a war movie, your busy brain replays the deep-seated knowledge that you cannot kill yourself in a simulator. You most definitely can while landing on a carrier at night. But that's what training does for you. It gives you the ability to apply reason to primal fear. When your brain says, "We can do this," the rest of you goes along.

Barnyard and I got four arrested landings (traps) that night, as well as four catapult launches (cat shots). The people, the machinery, the orchestrated symphony of deck activity were the same as during the day. But on the carrier deck, the blanket of darkness was pushed back by strange orange lights—orange, because that color interferes the least with the night vision of our eyes. We did not use night vision devices for carrier landings, so seeing everything in orange added a surreal feeling to the experience.

Surreal is not a strong enough word to describe the experience of calmly flying around a pitch-black sky for an hour, steadily monitoring red-lit instruments, breathing oxygen through a mask, talking on the radio and occasionally trading small talk or mission-related comments with your pilot. We really could have been sitting in a black room. Until the final two minutes of greatly increased activity and stress, followed by the physically jarring arrested landing that suddenly placed us on a small world dimly lit by orange lights. In this place we talked to each other and interacted with people outside for a frenzied few moments until we were again brain-scrambled by a cat shot into the serenity of darkness. This time it was only a few minutes of serenity before we again started the relentless rush of a night carrier approach.

No, surreal is *not* a strong enough word.

As I write this, separated from the events by decades of perspective and thousands of flight hours since, I enjoy the recollection of entering and then mastering that world. Within a few months, I was feeling totally comfortable on a carrier flight deck, day or night. Soon I was amazed at how much more information I could process during night carrier approaches. I never took these operations for granted; I could always hear that background music. But like my fellow carrier aviators, I became comfortable with the job.

Barnyard and I logged 3.0 hours of flight time that night. It had been a full day. As we climbed away from the ship after our final trap and cat, the RAG LSOs radioed with a terse but welcome message: "You're a qual."

"All right!" Barnyard blurted out over the radio. He probably felt like lighting the burners and doing a few victory rolls as we punched through layers of clouds. So did I, but we kept our emotions in check.

It was late when we landed at Oceana and debriefed. The night had gone smoothly, so the discussion was fairly short. As with our day traps, the LSO comments were relayed to us so we could get the most training benefit from the experience.

The overwhelming sense was that we had successfully cleared one of the biggest hurdles of our training: qualifying for carrier ops. I was on the verge of completing the RAG and reporting to a Fleet F-14 squadron. Barnyard, an LSO himself, would remain at the RAG as an instructor.

I wasn't scheduled on Wednesday, so I slept late. The day off was a welcome rest after the intensity of the past few days—actually, the past few weeks—of training. I joined up with a few of my classmates who had also completed their quals, and we all went out for beers.

On Thursday I was scheduled for a bonus flight with one of the more senior RAG instructors, the operations officer. He had been flying F-14s for several years, ever since they were new, and had logged hundreds of carrier landings, so he didn't need any traps for qualification. He was hoping that there would be a gap in the essential activity on *Nimitz* so he could get some bonus landings—that's known as "bagging traps." I liked the impromptu nature of the flight, and it wouldn't be a graded event for me.

We suited up, launched, and flew out to the carrier. We checked in and were sent to a holding pattern, where we monitored flight deck activity on our second radio. Having lost some time early in the week due to bad weather, and with other aircraft to qualify in addition to our F-14s, the whole operation was behind schedule. After two hours we realized the quest for extra traps was futile and returned to Oceana. There was no down side; I got to spend a couple more hours flying in a Tomcat.

Since I had flown over on the airlift, I was at the top of the list to fly an F-14 back to Miramar—my preferred way to travel. I knew I would gain some more experience in dealing with the different air traffic control agencies and situations that emerged during flights. Although I'd been flying Tomcats for six months and had more than seventy flight hours, it was still a new and exhilarating experience. And, as with the flight to bag traps, the return flights to Miramar wouldn't be graded!

We were paired with another Tomcat for the trip, which would be flown by Sandy Winnefeld and his RIO, Flash Gordon. Using the charts in the Oceana Base Operations planning room, we planned a route that would carry us fairly straight across the country. The wall map of the continental United States was speckled with suitable places to land and refuel. Almost any naval air station or air force base would do, and in 1981 we had many choices (more than we would now). The longest leg was our first, just over 900 miles, from Oceana to Little Rock AFB in Arkansas. Even without external fuel tanks, our jets had the range to fly further, but with shorter legs we wouldn't have to worry about fuel.

We filed our flight plan, put on our gear, and launched into the clear blue late morning sky, the best weather we'd seen since arriving in Virginia Beach. Once we climbed to altitude we spread out into loose formation. Tomcats had flown well above 50,000 feet in testing, but on flights like these we normally stayed at more modest altitudes in the high twenties or low thirties. Test Tomcats had also flown more than 1,600 mph, but flying faster uses fuel faster. To get the range we wanted, we often flew at about 550 mph (roughly 0.8 Mach)—about as fast as an airliner.

Still, we were reminded that we were flying one of the latest and hottest jets around. One incredulous air traffic controller asked, "Navy November Juliet 430, confirm your aircraft type as Fox-Fourteen." Another forwarded a comment from a passing airliner: "Navy 447, United 216 says you guys are looking good today."

I kept my replies simple. Yes, we were indeed Tomcats, and "Navy 447 copies, thanks." Anything more would have sounded cheesy.

It was a comfortable ride, especially for a fighter. Our cockpits were roomy, the air conditioning was strong, and the panoramic canopy gave us an incredible view. But we were strapped into thinly padded ejection seats, so after a couple of hours it felt good to get out and stretch when we landed at Little Rock. We grabbed sandwiches at the flight line cafeteria while our jets were being refueled, and in about forty minutes we were back in the air for the short flight to Cannon AFB in Clovis, New Mexico, 630 miles from Little Rock.

We decided to fly this leg at a higher altitude, and were cleared to 40,000 feet and higher, where the sky became a dark blue-gray. With the relaxed formation of cross-country cruising, Barnyard slipped directly below Sandy and Flash. Suddenly their Tomcat eclipsed the sun and flashed a prismatic corona in the thin layer of clouds, which were probably crystals of ice in the cold of high altitude. I asked Barnyard to do it again while I pulled out my camera and took one of the few photos I shot during the entire week. When I had it printed, I knew it was a keeper.

We made a quick stop at Cannon AFB for fuel and took off for the 810-mile trip to Miramar, arriving Saturday afternoon. Our CQ adventure was over, and ten pilots and RIOs were now carrier-qualified in the F-14. We were nearing the end of our time at VF-124.

I was scheduled for a single event the following week, a classroom lecture on Friday. The week after that I had my last flight in the RAG, a 2v2 that was not particularly memorable. I'd like to think I displayed the brilliance of a future Topgun instructor, but I think my performance on that final flight would have to be described as "adequate."

As we neared the end of our time at VF-124, an instructor told us we had a week to think about squadrons we wanted to be assigned to, and to list our top three choices. There were about eight F-14 squadrons at Miramar, along with a few squadrons still flying the F-4 Phantom. Paul, Steve, and I tried to be methodical. We considered which squadrons were just returning from deployment and thus would spend the most time at home before deploying again; which ones had brand-new jets fresh from the Grumman factory; which ones fit any criteria that seemed sensible. Several of us walked around to the various ready rooms, looking for insight or inspiration. At last we filled in the forms with our top choices and turned them in.

I don't know whether our RAG instructors glanced at our requests before throwing them away, or just threw them away immediately. In this matter we were a commodity, and larger forces determined which squadrons needed new pilots and RIOs. I was assigned to VF-24, the "Fighting Renegades." VF-24 wasn't even on my list.

VF-24 was in the second wave of squadrons to make the switch to F-14s, receiving their first Tomcats in December 1975. They were, of course based at Miramar, as virtually every student who completed VF-124 went to a Miramar F-14 squadron. When VF-24 made operational deployments, it was assigned to USS *Constellation*, which was stationed at NAS North Island. This would prove convenient, as North Island was in the scenic town of Coronado, an easy twenty-mile drive from Miramar. Several carriers were based near San Francisco or Washington State, and every time their assigned squadrons moved on and off, for training or overseas deployment, they had to contend with trips of five hundred or more than a thousand miles.

I was not going to VF-24 alone. My buddies Paul and Gary, and fellow Georgia Tech alumnus Sandy—these and other RAG classmates went to VF-24. Other RAG classmates were ordered to VF-211, which was the other F-14 squadron assigned to *Constellation*, so I would see them regularly for the next few years. The other members of our class went to other squadrons at Miramar and I rarely saw them again, save for chance meetings at the O-Club.

Around the same time as we were considering which squadron we wanted, RAG instructors told us to start thinking about something less formal, but no less important: our own personal callsigns. In most aviation squadrons, callsigns were used as nicknames, though they were never called that. They were an aviator's *nom de guerre*, a way to contact him over the radio without revealing his true identity, or without causing confusion if there were several people named John (or Jake in more recent times) in the air at the same time. A callsign was another way to bond warriors together, and once bestowed they were used at all times. In fact, callsigns basically replaced given names. So they were not to be taken lightly.

From our experience with instructors in Pensacola and the RAG, we knew callsigns could fall into many categories. Quite a few guys from Texas were known as Cowboy or Tex, and many squadrons had a Snake. Heroic callsigns, such as Eagle, Shark, or Killer, were relatively rare. Comedic and insulting were more common, such as Flounder or Spaz. Many callsigns were based on last names—"Ice" Berg and "Dream" Weaver. And of course some were downright naughty.... Use your imagination.

Many students, close to completing the F-14 RAG and joining the Fleet, considered themselves in the heroic or menacing category. For example, they would write Shark on the board in a flight brief, only to be mocked by the instructors, who changed the board to read Minnow. I often wondered why the instructors even asked us what we wanted as our callsigns. Even after a callsign was attached to an aviator, a single incident early in their career was enough to change a callsign, if it was good enough. Or usually bad enough.

When I had a few minutes to address this weighty problem, I sought the counsel of LT Steve "Superman" Jones, an instructor RIO who was known as a good guy and straight shooter. And as Superman, he obviously knew something about callsigns, and how to get a good one. I decided to try to get a clever callsign based on my last name. My family always pronounced Baranek to rhyme with "bionic." This was only a few years after the TV show *The Six Million Dollar Man,* so bionic was a common term. Ignoring the fact that I wasn't actually very bionic, Superman encouraged me to go with that. You can look at the cover of the book and see that Bionic was shortened to Bio, and that was the callsign I kept.

Over the years, as I encountered the wide range of callsigns that my fellow aviators bore, I decided that Bio wasn't bad.

And then along came a guy called Streak. About the middle of my time in the RAG I started to notice a lieutenant who was always hurrying through the squadron. He was one of many officers who had completed a tour in an F-14 squadron, then served another assignment, and was back at the RAG for a re-qual. That intermediate assignment had a big impact on how demanding it was for these aviators to re-qualify. This guy was a pilot, and it seemed like he was already up to speed. So he'd just pop into the ready room to check on a flight, run through the snack bar where we sometimes hung out, and occasionally sit in on a class. Every time he came by, instructors would say something like, "Hey, Streak, how's it going?" This guy Streak was a celeb, and everybody seemed to know him.

One day we asked one of the instructors about Streak, and he said, "Oh, he just finished his tour as a Topgun instructor." Now we knew why Streak seemed to breeze through the training that was so challenging for us. Topgun was the Navy's elite school for its best fighter pilots and RIOs, and to be an instructor there, you had to be better than the best.

"He's here for re-qual," the instructor added. "Then he goes back to the Fleet. I think he's going to VF-24." All right, that's my new squadron!

Streak turned out to be LT Marty Chanik. Later he told me that he got the callsign Streak because he had a patch of light hair on his head full of otherwise black hair. You'll read more about him in a few pages.

My last day in the RAG was Monday, April 13, 1981, eight months after I'd started. Back then, it really didn't matter much whether I went to VF-24, VF-1, VF-111, or some other squadron. I was a moldable, enthusiastic young naval officer and would do my best wherever I went. But now I think back at how events unfolded and built upon each other, and I see that I was very fortunate indeed to be assigned to VF-24. Events that would shape my life started to happen just a few months after my arrival.

But that is another story. It's in a book called *Topgun Days*. Meantime, read a few of my stories about flying in the Fleet.

SPECIAL SECTION

# Flying in the Fleet

I wasn't called "student" anymore. I was about to fly with a Fleet fighter squadron.

I'd been released from the structure of the training environment. There was no instructor looking over my shoulder or grading me in classroom and cockpit or backing me up when I blew it. I was expected to perform as a qualified and responsible member of the team. For people in a complex and dangerous job, there is no better feeling than knowing you can depend on your teammates.

There was a culture of professionalism in the squadron—in *every* squadron—and I was prepared for it. But in the Fleet you never stop preparing. There were still regular tests and check-flights, still briefings and debriefings, still missions to keep that combat readiness honed to a razor edge.

Squadron duty proved to be a richer and more rewarding experience than I had imagined.

Here are four glimpses of what lay ahead.

# Flying in the Fleet—Carrier Landing Emergency Leads to Airborne Divert

USS *Constellation* left San Diego on Tuesday, October 20, 1981, and headed into the Pacific for a seven and a half month deployment. There were no conflicts involving American forces. This was a normal peacetime operation, demonstrating US interests, exercising with partner nations, patrolling the seas. We didn't fly for the first few days as the ship powered west at high speed. By October 25 we were a few hundred miles from Hawaii, so we started flight ops. The ship's last flight ops had been a little more than a month before, and we needed to "knock off the rust." Soon we would be flying in the open ocean, hundreds of miles from land, but for the first few days it was important to have a land base that we could divert to in case of emergency. On that first day, I had a 9:00 a.m. briefing for a low-stress flight to get everyone into the mindset. That was followed by a 4:00 p.m. brief for a routine night flight, mainly to re-qualify pilots who had not made a night carrier landing in more than a month.

We flew some radar intercepts to pass the time with a little training until the main event: carrier landings and quals to refresh the pilots' skills. All aircraft went to holding early to conserve fuel. The ship directed us one by one to begin our approaches.

One of the first planes to land that night was an A-7 Corsair II attack jet. It hit the deck hard and blew both main landing gear tires. The exploding tires threw chunks of rubber all over the landing area. This type of development was only a minor mishap. It wasn't exactly common, but it happened every few months. The hard rubber of aircraft tires would damage any jet engines that ingested it, so the carrier's crew scurried to move the hobbled aircraft and clear the landing area of debris.

Connie's controllers radioed "Delta easy," the signal to be as conservative as possible with fuel. In my five months of carrier ops, I had heard this a few times and knew things could go either way: The problem could be solved quickly, or we might be in for some challenges. I was still relatively new at this and took comfort in flying with an experienced pilot, LT John "John Boy" Alling, who had been in the squadron for two years and already completed one deployment. Typical of Fleet squadrons, first-cruise RIOs normally flew with experienced pilots, and first-cruise pilots had a more experienced RIO.

In a few minutes the Air Boss himself came on the radio—a rare event—and reported that they were cleaning up the mess and we should resume landings in fifteen minutes. Like every other person flying, John Boy and I calculated our fuel situation and gave ourselves pats on the back for being conservative. Fifteen extra minutes? No problem.

Yes, problem. About ten minutes later the Boss radioed again and said there were some problems clearing the deck, and the expected delay was another thirty minutes. He told all aircraft to check in and report their fuel state. We all listened to each other and thought the same thing: still no problem. We had all been cautious and saved fuel, planning to dump it during the last few miles of our approach to landing. Aircraft had already launched for the late-night event after ours, and they included aerial tankers, but it was decided to hold the tankers for the aircraft just launched and we were told we would not be able to aerial refuel.

It's important to know that all carrier-based aircraft have a maximum weight for carrier landings, known as "max trap." This is based on limiting stress on the aircraft and its components, but in the case of the F-14 it was also based on the maximum weight that the ship's arresting gear could handle. The basic weight of the aircraft could not be changed in flight, and it was not realistic to reduce weight by getting rid of missiles or fuel tanks, as this would quickly become very expensive. So the way we adjusted weight to meet max trap was by adjusting fuel.*

* As an example based on realistic weights, the max trap for an F-14 was 51,800 pounds. A typical F-14A aircraft weighed 45,000 pounds empty, with missile carrying rails and other fixed equipment. For a training mission we may carry three missiles with a total weight of 1,700 pounds, giving us a figure of 46,700 pounds to work with. This meant we could have no more than 5,100 pounds of fuel when landing on the carrier (46,700 plus 5,100 equals 51,800). Later, improved arresting gear could accept F-14s at 54,000 pounds, which allowed them to carry more weapons on routine flights and land with more fuel, both of which were nice developments. The real-time mental math that started in Pensacola never ended.

About 45 minutes after the tires blew, the tone of voices changed as pilots and RIOs updated their fuel states and inquired about the cleanup. The situation was getting critical. John Boy told me to get out my reference booklets and look up our divert field: Naval Air Station Barbers Point, outside Honolulu. We had enough fuel to wait a little longer and still fly to the field, so I wasn't worried. But a few minutes later came the first call from a plane telling the ship they were at a decision point. Connie said the expected delay was fifteen more minutes, so the aircrew wisely decided to divert to Barbers Point.

As soon as one pilot made that decision, the rest of us quickly did the same.

I switched my radio to Honolulu air traffic control and heard a pack of Navy planes. When there was an opening in communication I checked in. I reported our position and soon the controller located us on his radar and gave initial instructions. By the Tomcat's built-in flashlight, I read the navigation chart. Since this was a field we had never used before, John Boy relied on me to describe the conditions and course rules for approaching aircraft. We could see the lights of Honolulu from 100 miles away in the total blackness of the Pacific. We flew through scattered and well-defined clouds as we neared the field, descending, switching frequencies, following navigation instructions, and listening to the other diverting aircraft doing the same.

Soon we were on deck at Barbers Point. Since there was no plane captain to meet us when we reached a parking area, John Boy shut down the left engine and I climbed out of the cockpit. I walked along the spine of the plane, sat down on the horizontal tail and slid to the end, then dropped about five feet to the ground. I opened a storage box tucked in the nose landing gear well to retrieve some metal pins, then inserted them in critical joints in the landing gear to make sure it wouldn't collapse when we shut down the plane. This is a precaution taken on every aircraft with retractable gear, but normally done by the PC. I gave John Boy a thumbs-up and he shut down the second engine. We had flown for 3.5 hours.

Another Tomcat pulled in next to us and I ran over, got their attention, and installed their gear pins. It was our XO and his RIO. The rest of the diverting aircraft soon landed and taxied over. There were about six planes. To their credit, Barbers Point sent a truck out to give us a ride to the officers quarters.

It was about 10 p.m. We assessed who had made this divert and determined VF-24 XO Commander Bertsch was the senior officer, so he went to the base control tower and contacted the ship by radio. Meanwhile we arrived at the officers quarters—which was like a dorm or budget motel—and decided it would be nice to spend a night *not* on our ship. So we went to the beer vending machine and each bought a beer. This would be our excuse that we could not fly back that night, since it was illegal to fly for eight hours after drinking even one beer. (The rules have since become even more restrictive.)

The XO—the executive officer, second in command of the squadron—arrived at the quarters a few minutes later and grabbed a beer himself. The ship was just finishing cleaningup the landing area, he said, and had their hands full recovering the event that launched after us, so they did not want us back that night anyway. Instead we were to launch the next day and be at the ship at 1 p.m. So we ordered pizza and played cards, and most guys got another beer.

The next day was one of those incredibly bright tropical days with beautiful clouds. Barbers Point personnel had refueled our jets and we launched about noon. John Boy and I flew on the XO's wing to simplify the air traffic control problem, while controllers directed us to the area where *Constellation* was operating and we contacted Connie when we were 100 miles from the ship. We had been written into the ship's schedule, to land with the 1:15 p.m. recovery—very efficient. Each type of aircraft was assigned a mission and told to switch to a radio frequency. We switched to our assigned frequency and contacted another VF-24 aircraft that had launched to work with us.

Since we had not conducted a detailed brief we flew a training mission that we could do with minimal coordination: 2v1 short setups. Two Tomcats would act as the fighter section, while the third aircraft was the bogey. Instead of thirty miles or more, the intercepts were a maximum of twenty miles.

The short setup was great because the RIOs acting as "fighters" had a dynamic radar problem of detecting the bogey, ensuring both aircraft had radar contact, directing the intercept to gain position advantage, and talking the pilots to a sighting of the bogey (*tally-ho* or just *tally*). On the other side, the bogey Tomcat had valuable training at detecting two aircraft and making sure both RIO and pilot had sight of the fighters at the merge. We would continue through only 180-degree of turn before the knock-it-off call, then switch partners and fly away from each other until we saw 20 miles of separation on our TACAN navigation instrument. As we approached 20 miles the bogey would call, "Turning in, fight's on" to begin the next run.

Since the XO and John Boy were in formation flying out from Barbers Point, we were the first fighters. I'd done this before, and always enjoyed the fast pace of 2v1 short set-ups. On this day the bright clouds—as well-defined as white puffy mountains—provided a grand arena for our combat. For nearly an hour it was: "204 turning in, fight's on." "Contact 15 left, 18 miles, come left 330." "Tally left 11 low." "Fox two." "Knock it off, 210 outbound as the bogey." Then, less than four minutes after last turn-in: "210 turning in, fight's on." "Contact 5 right, 17 miles, come right 010." And that was just the communication over the radio; there was more over the ICS.

We flew ten or twelve runs before we had to stop to make our landing time. We flew to the day holding pattern overhead *Constellation* and watched the launch of the next event. When the deck was clear we descended, swept our wings back, entered the break, turned downwind and spread the wings, and came in for our landings.

Flight ops in the vicinity of Hawaii on a carrier headed west...we were really on deployment.

# Flying in the Fleet—Single-Engine Carrier Landing

In December 1981, I had been in VF-24 about six months. I was flying with Streak for a midday ACM flight, a 1v1 close-in dogfight against Holly as pilot and Rums as RIO. Holly was LT Fred Hollinger, who was on his second overseas deployment with VF-24 and as such was one of the senior lieutenants. USS *Constellation* was in the South China Sea headed toward Singapore, hundreds of miles from any land airbases. It was a clear and bright day like most days on deployment. That's the way it is in the tropics, and when the weather is bad the carrier goes to where the weather is good.

We had started with low-speed maneuvers to burn fuel so we would not put excessive stress on the jets when we began the hard maneuvering engagements. Based on fuel load, we would be limited to 6 g. First full ACM engagement would be 1v1 with a neutral setup: both Tomcats flying the same heading, at an altitude of 20,000 feet and speed of 350 knots.

Streak and I were steady on a heading of 270 degrees with Holly and Rums on our left side, 1½ miles away. This is one of the standard training setups for 1v1 ACM. We still had a lot of time in the flight and had to manage our fuel, so the first fight was mil-power only, no afterburner. A close engagement in a Tomcat without using burner is completely different from the typical full-on dogfight. So this was great training for the pilots, who had to carefully manage airspeed to keep the plane maneuverable.

I checked with my pilot, then radioed, "Streak's ready." Rums replied, "Holly's ready." I said, "Recorders on, fight's on."

Rums and I punched the Record buttons on the mini-cassette tape recorders we had wired into our communications gear. These tapes would help reconstruct the fight during debrief.

Streak pulled the nose up slightly and started a hard 6 g left turn, then after gaining a small advantage (called "getting a bite") allowed our nose to fall below the horizon to maintain our speed. The Tomcat could easily pull more g, but was limited to 6.5 g maximum so the aircraft would not be overstressed.

I reached to my right and activated the auto-lock radar mode, but we were too close and it did not lock. We passed about 700 feet from Holly and continued in our nose-low turn to the left. Holly continued his right turn and reduced his rate of descent. It was a calculated move: he was now trying to gain altitude advantage. Okay, I thought, we're starting a one-circle fight. This was going to involve constant g-loads.

How many times had Holly done this in more than two years of flying Tomcats, including five weeks at the Topgun class?

How many times had Streak fought similar fights, with over a thousand hours flying Tomcats? How many times had he faced this situation in his two and a half years as a Topgun Instructor?

And how lucky was I to be part of this "clash of the titans"?

Streak and I watched over our left shoulders as Holly directed his Tomcat into an intimidating position, but it was a fleeting accomplishment and he did not get a shot. Soon he was slow and had to come down, while Streak had preserved enough airspeed to maintain an altitude advantage.

And so we fought through several passes in the clear tropical air. The small puffy clouds and crystal blue ocean provided the backdrop for the engagement. Both pilots called a missile shot or two—shots they would have taken in combat—but we continued the fight because none of them was a decisive "kill shot."

As the fight continued and we descended in altitude, I kept up with RIO duties in a 1v1 training engagement. I frequently reported airspeed to Streak so he could keep his eyes on the target. I operated the radar when the target approached the auto-lock zones, checked fuel every few seconds against our fuel plan, carefully watched altitude, and performed dozens of other tasks including taking notes.

After a few turns we passed through 10,000-foot altitude and the pilots adhered to the restriction against low-speed maneuvering. In a few more turns we descended to 5,000 feet above the ocean—not especially low, but this was the altitude at which ACM ceased for safety reasons. Both pilots were acutely aware of altitude as we descended. It would be interesting to see a re-creation of the dogfight as it evolved from a three-dimensional spiral to a series of flat circles just above 5,000 feet. This was common for a 1v1, so in a few seconds Holly called, "Knock it off." There was no need to use more gas in a nearly stagnant situation.

Streak said, "Knock it off, Streak is 10.2," reporting our fuel state. Holly started to climb back up to start the next fight. Streak selected afterburner to increase our speed and climb quicker.

Our right engine failed immediately.

Our Tomcat lurched as the full thrust of the left engine pushed that side of the aircraft forward. The nose jerked to the right. Things happened fast. Streak pulled both throttles back out of burner. With stick and rudder he coaxed the jet back under control. I said, "Lock your harness," one of the first boldface steps for a departure (which this felt like the start of), and checked our altitude.

We were back in stable flight in just a second.

Holly came up on the private radio frequency we were using and said, "You got it?" and Streak said, "We're okay."

"Wow," said Rums, "you should have seen the flame that came out of your right engine!"

Our right engine had destroyed itself. When all that fuel for afterburner squirted into the dying engine, it exploded in a billowing sheet of yellow flame more than thirty feet long. The normal burner plume was almost invisible in the daytime since it burned hot, but a failed engine plume is a very visible bright yellow. Rums later said he thought about asking us to try it again so he could get a photo. Joking? I wonder...

ACM was over for this flight. We were in a fighter designed for two engines but flying now with one. We assessed our situation and notified the ship. A single-engine Tomcat was not that unusual, and our situation was stable, so they launched the next event on schedule. Since we were far from land, and all of our repair assets were aboard the ship, our options added up to exactly one: a single-engine approach to *Constellation*.

Instead of the normal overhead position, however, we were told to orbit at a unique point ten miles from the ship. Holly stayed on our wing as escort. Tomcats normally landed first, but now all other aircraft on our event landed before us. For a very good reason: If we had a problem or crashed, fourteen planes low on fuel would be stranded up in the air.

The approach was anticlimactic, which is what you want when dealing with expensive flammable objects and human lives. It's also a reward for good training. Streak was very careful with the one good throttle and the LSOs on the ship were in "emergency mode." They considered our less-than-normal thrust in evaluating our approach, plus they were extra calm on the radios—which always helps in emergencies. They actually made just a single call as we neared the carrier, because Streak flew an incredibly smooth and stable approach. We landed without incident.

When debriefing him on the landing, they said it looked like he was "on rails."

Holly and Rums made a tight downwind turn and trapped a few seconds after we were clear of the landing area. Later that day our jet engine mechanics determined that something—a stray bolt?—had gotten into the engine and caused some damage. The engine operated okay until the full-power stress of afterburner caused catastrophic failure. It happens. We handled the problem quickly and things remained stable until we landed. Streak did the hard work, and for me it never got scary. And Rums never got his photo.

# Flying in the Fleet—Supersonic AIM-7 Missile Exercise

December 1982, NAS Miramar. I'd been in my Fleet squadron, the VF-24 Fighting Renegades, for more than a year and a half, and had completed a seven and a half month overseas deployment.

As part of the normal program of training aircrews and verifying weapon system effectiveness, Lieutenant Commander Steve "Drifty" Smith and I were selected to launch an AIM-7 "Sparrow" missile at a target over the Pacific Ocean off Southern California. This would be the second time I shot an actual AIM-7 at a target drone since I joined the VF-24 Fighting Renegades. In our dogfight training events we simply called missile shots over the radio. Actually launching a missile was much more complex than the pilot squeezing the trigger or the RIO pushing a button. That's why we had these exercises.

Our aircraft would carry two AIM-7 missiles, in case there was a problem with one, and two AIM-9 Sidewinders to finish off the target if necessary—all standard procedure.

I was excited to be scheduled for a MISSILEX—a missile exercise, with its challenge of managing the F-14's weapon system from start to finish. It began with aviation fire control technicians prepping the radar, and aviation ordnance men loading the missiles. Then it was up to the pilot and RIO to put our aircraft into the correct missile launch zone, and get a radar lock that would guide the twelve-foot-long Sparrow to the target. But this shot would include extra challenges, as it was a "test and evaluation" (T&E) profile, requiring that we and the target both fly supersonic, and also requiring us to launch at a specific range and approach angle to the target. Instead of the explosive warhead fired in combat, ours had a telemetry package to send information to engineers on the ground.

We would approach the target about twice as fast as on most training intercepts, so I had to closely watch the radar and carefully control the run. If you've never run supersonic intercepts, let me tell you that things move much faster than they do during typical training intercepts, when both fighter and target are flying at 350 knots (400 mph) or so. That may seem obvious. But there must be a calculation, something like stress equals the square of the speed. So, even though I had been in a front-line squadron more than eighteen months, we practiced for the shoot with a few runs in the F-14 simulator. No one wanted us to mess this up.

The firing run happened about 4 p.m. on a Wednesday afternoon, in designated airspace over the ocean 100 miles west of Los Angeles. We were scheduled to shoot at an AQM-37 target drone launched from an A-6 Intruder operated by the Pacific Missile Test Center. Drifty and I waited a few minutes at an assigned station at the southern end of the range, at an altitude of 23,000 feet, and when everything was ready we headed north. I spotted the A-6 on radar at around eighty miles, which agreed with the calls we were getting from our controller. I started to feel comfortable.

Military forces have used unmanned air vehicles as targets since the early 1900s. Today they are known as unmanned aerial vehicles or systems (UAV or UAS), but an unofficial term used in the 1980s was "drone." Drones are good targets for air-to-air missiles, and there are few alternatives. On some MISSILEXes, the drone controller would make a hard turn an instant after the missile was launched in an attempt to cause a miss, allowing the drone to be recovered and used again. Reusing the drone was more achievable because many missiles launched for training did not have an explosive warhead that would destroy a target in the event of a near miss instead of a direct hit. Other times, the target drone was considered expendable and a warhead-equipped missile would destroy it, providing a spectacular view to the aircrew. Drones are available in many types: some are relatively simple, jet-propelled, and subsonic—essentially small aircraft. The AQM-37 in this story was fourteen feet long and rocket powered, giving it supersonic capability. Many retired fighter aircraft have even been converted into unmanned targets.

As we approached the launch range, Drifty shoved the throttles to max burner and we accelerated through Mach 1. I thought about how little drama there was to it. If I hadn't looked at the airspeed indicator I wouldn't have noticed when we went supersonic. The A-6 reported launching the drone, which was powered by a rocket engine, and seconds later I detected it as a new target when it accelerated far ahead. The A-6 made a hard 180-degree turn to leave the area—can't blame him!—and we commenced the firing run. Our range to the target was thirty miles. That may sound like a long distance, but we were supersonic and so was the drone. Add the two speeds, and you find that the range was shrinking by more than two thousand feet *each second*. In afterburner at this altitude, we were burning a thousand pounds of jet fuel every minute.

I was working with Drifty to carefully manage our approach: "Come right ten degrees." "Now back to three-five-zero (degrees)." "Climb to 28,000." He was also helping by reading the info on his repeat display up front. Even though RIOs were responsible for intercept control, pilots knew how to run intercepts, and Drifty had been a RAG instructor, so he was great in a tough situation.

One minute after the start, we were at the right range and angle to launch the Sparrow. I pushed the red "missile launch" button. The 500-pound weapon jumped off the jet with a strong *thump*—that was the small explosive charges that made sure it cleared the plane—and rocketed out ahead of us.

I told Drifty to make a hard right turn. I had hesitated for a second or two, and I knew I could be in trouble.

As we made our turn I looked at the small scope in front of my face and watched the target blip drift toward the left side. As it neared the edge of the screen I told Drifty to come back left in a hard turn, and regretted my hesitation. I had been running intercepts almost three years, but at these speeds things were happening fast. Drifty rolled the jet left to 90 degrees and put on a good pull. We were doing Mach 1.1 and pulling about 5 g. Slicing through the evening sky with our wings swept all the way back at 68 degrees and the burners ablaze, we would have looked really cool if there had been anyone around to see us.

I sweated the radar picture. I had two small green lights indicating the radar was still locked on the drone. But the track was near the edge of my scope. If it went off the scope, that meant the radar antenna could not turn enough to follow the target. Our radar would break lock, the AIM-7 would "go stupid," and I would have to try to find that little drone again. That was hard enough when fighter and target were going 300 knots or less; at over 600 knots . . . I didn't want to think about it.

Halfway through the turn my "radar lock" lights went out. I had messed up the intercept! "Broke lock," I growled to Drifty. "Going to search." I didn't have to include the *dammit!* that I was thinking.

"Bio, relax," Drifty drawled. "It was a direct hit. We broke lock because the target is gone. We just blew it out of the sky."

Direct hit! Even without an explosive warhead, the Sparrow hit the drone at Mach 3 and created a small explosion in the afternoon sky. I didn't see it, but I enjoyed it nonetheless.

# Flying in the Fleet—Project "Rising Fighter"

This episode also takes place in December 1982, an exciting time for me with some great flying. I'd been in the Fleet (VF-24) for twenty months and had about 800 flight hours in the F-14—a good amount of experience. More importantly for this story, it was only two months after completing the Topgun class. I was invited to participate in a series of flights for a research project, and my pilot would be the same one I flew with in Topgun: Jaws. We had honed our crew coordination to a sharp edge during challenging scenarios fighting the Topgun instructors. Now we would get another chance to practice our craft. (I'm including this story to show how far my capabilities had progressed since I left the RAG, the value of experience on top of a solid foundation of training.)

The research flights were part of a project in which Miramar squadrons explored tactics against the new MiG-23 "Flogger." MiG-23s were more capable than MiG-17s and MiG-21s in some important respects: better radars, better missiles, and great top speed capability. They were very good interceptors, and in fact they were one of the first threat aircraft types that could launch missiles at US aircraft during the radar intercept, so they presented a major increase in the threat. A limitation was their relatively poor maneuverability. In the early 1980s Floggers were becoming fairly common in the air forces of potential enemies, and this ability to launch missiles at us before the merge caused real concern because it was the first time we faced this possibility.

The research project was called "Rising Fighter."

Rising Fighter consisted of 2vUNK scenarios: two Tomcats ran intercepts against an unknown number (UNK) of F-4 Phantoms from regular Navy squadrons. During the intercepts, all jets could use their radar and simulate launching missiles, and effective launches would be scored as kills. Any surviving aircraft would engage in a dogfight when the opposing formations met. It was an all-out, aggressive scenario that would require Jaws and I to use all of our skills.

We flew all runs on the instrumented Tactical Aircrew Combat Training System (TACTS) Range near Yuma, with high quality intercept control and real-time kill removal. That meant that a good missile shot by either the fighters (Tomcats) or the bogeys (Phantoms) resulted in an aircraft being called "dead" and immediately disengaging. Based on tactical thinking at the time, we Tomcats used only Sparrow and Sidewinder missiles, the same as the Phantoms.

These missiles were roughly similar to a Flogger's missiles, so our F-14s had little advantage in this category.

Eight weeks after we finished Topgun, Jaws and I joined Cowboy and Ice (the pilot and RIO from VF-24, flying the other F-14) for a week of Rising Fighter. We flew one flight per day for five days. The Phantom pilots and RIOs were not Topgun instructors, but several of them had been through the class. F-4 Phantoms provided a good simulation of many Flogger characteristics, at least for the purposes of this exercise. No restrictions were placed on tactics used by either side, so we were facing well-trained US Navy pilots and RIOs. The missiles that both sides launched would be simulated, but as the Phantom neared the end of twenty-five years as a front-line fighter with the US Navy, its aircrews wanted to show they still had it. Meanwhile, we Tomcat crews wanted to demonstrate the superiority of our still-new fighter.

In these 2vUNK runs we were always outnumbered. Our primary advantages were our better radar to help us develop situational awareness (SA) during the intercept, and our superior maneuverability once we got to the merge. The hard part was getting there. These guys could shoot us in the face and kill us.

Most flights included at least two intercepts to engagements, and the odds were 2v4, 2v5, or 2v6. But that was only how the intercept started. With the aggressive pre-merge shots and kills, both sides suffered casualties. For me, Rising Fighter was just the right challenge. We would start a run, the radar picture would show five bogeys, and I would think, *bring it*.

Seared into my memory forever are snapshot images from a flight that started as a 2v6 and turned into a long

1v5 engagement. On the intercept, the Tomcats killed one Phantom—this was a positive for us. But Cowboy was kill-removed just before the merge, leaving Jaws and me to fight five Phantoms. It was a day with a high layer of thick clouds, softening the browns and grays of the desert during those microseconds I registered the terrain for orientation. We were flying about 450 knots when we merged with the Phantoms, and they were the same, maybe faster. I had used my radar effectively to describe their formation, and Jaws started seeing them at eight miles. "Tally two F-4s. Looking for the others."

As we flashed past their formation at 1,000 knots closing speed, Jaws immediately cranked our jet into a crushing 6.5-g left turn to get into position to take the first shots. He said, "Watch the guys on the right!" The Phantoms scattered out of their formation.

"Tally three. No threat," I replied.

Through my visor I noticed our wings, with the high-lift leading edge slats deployed, tremble under high g forces and turbulent airflow while we stressed our fighter in max-performance turns. At that fuel state we weighed more than twenty-five tons.

It wasn't easy, but Jaws and I were in our element. We had refreshed the "contracts" we developed when we went through the Topgun class, such as who looked forward and who looked back. Our weapons system use and inter-cockpit comms were spot-on, based on practice, candid debriefs, and constant improvement. We used every system available in our Tomcat. In my general experience, use of the radar warning equipment had not been emphasized, but it was a priority for Jaws and me. I used a "bypass" function so it would alert us if an F-4's radar—which was categorized as friendly, not a threat—locked us up in preparation for a missile shot.

We pulled more than 6 g almost constantly in the fight, but this wasn't a problem after all of the dogfighting I had done in the past few months. Jaws called an AIM-9 Sidewinder missile shot on one Phantom and the controllers declared him killed, so he climbed away from the fight.

A moment later Jaws called an AIM-7 Sparrow on another Phantom. Another kill. We were now 1v3.

This memorable contest was a tight turning engagement approaching two minutes' duration. I had to suppress my inclination to watch the "dogfight action" over Jaws's shoulder; my responsibility was defensive lookout, behind us. Over my right shoulder I picked up a Phantom slicing through a descending turn, a few seconds from becoming a threat, as we pursued another Phantom through a left turn. Over the ICS I told Jaws, "Approaching, right four (o'clock) high. Okay, hard right."

As Jaws broke off his attack on the jet in front of us, the irritating screech from our warning equipment announced that the Phantom had taken a radar lock. He was about to launch a missile. I made an awkward reach with my right hand to launch a few rounds of decoy flares and chaff in anticipation of the shot. We used simulated missiles, but real chaff and flares. The chaff broke his radar lock as our hard right turn neutralized his approach. We traded updates on the F-4s remaining in the fight and Jaws returned to pursuing our original target. In a few more seconds he called another missile shot and we notched another kill.

Checking our fuel, we realized we needed to leave the area, to bug out. No Phantoms were threatening, so we headed to the southwest and extended out of their missile range. With radio calls of "Knock it off," the engagement was over.

In the context of Rising Fighter, it was just another event, a series of data points. When we returned to Miramar we reported the usual information—range of first radar detection, range at initial missile launch, etc.—and objectively debriefed the engagement.

But for me personally it has remains one of the more memorable missions from more than 3,000 hours of flying jet fighters.

# Epilogue

We humans have a priceless tool. It's called perspective. We can take events from the past and put them in context, reshape the story, and in telling it we can erase the embarrassing or trivial and concentrate on the positive. As I shaped the narrative for *Before Topgun Days*, I used perspective to select incidents and events to include, but I resisted glossing over the anxieties, difficulties, and mistakes. In fact, it is comfortable and amusing to look back and recall those feelings with full confidence in knowing that things turned out okay. More than okay; there were more rewards and adventures during my Navy flying career than I ever could have expected.

I've dropped hints about what came after I left VF-124, entered my Fleet squadron VF-24, and continued in my Navy career. That's in my book *Topgun Days*. The "highlights reel" would include the heart-stopping few seconds when I ejected from an F-14 Tomcat during a landing mishap aboard the carrier USS *Constellation* while flying with the commanding officer of VF-24, Commander Bill Switzer. That thrill ride demonstrated with crystal clarity the value of the training that began in Pensacola and continued every day of my life in the Fleet.

Another highlight was too long to fit on a highlights reel: five weeks as a student in the prestigious Topgun school. It was filled with incredible flying and learning as my pilot Jaws and I leaped forward in our ability to get the most out of the F-14 Tomcat.

Then came the dawning realization that I wanted to be an instructor at Topgun. I got my wish, and in the challenging and rewarding first months at Topgun I faced the intense instructor-under-training qualification program. There was also the amusing experience of working on the movie *Top Gun*, which became a cultural icon. Yes, I'm in it; I'm in the rear cockpit of the enemy MiG-28 "communicating" with Maverick.

There's much more in *Topgun Days*, along with larger topics such as life in a Navy fighter squadron, and two deployments with VF-24—seven and a half months each, traveling the world with five thousand of my closest friends, the crews of the aircraft carriers *Constellation* and *Ranger*. The flying, the port visits, the totality of the experience—is there a stronger word than "unforgettable"?

So, what happened after that? I followed the path of most Topgun instructors and returned to a Fleet F-14 squadron and two more overseas deployments. In VF-2, I learned a lot more about how a squadron operates through the ground jobs I was assigned—exactly what the Navy expects of officers at that stage in my career. As you would expect, I continued to learn and build my skill as an F-14 RIO during training and real-world operations. And I shot some of my favorite photos during that tour in VF-2.

At the end of that tour I was ready for the next phase of my career. The Navy, like the other military services, knows the value of "career broadening," serving outside your comfort zone to learn more of the big picture in the Navy or the Department of Defense. One way is to serve on the staff of a senior officer, and I was offered a prime position. So after more than ten years of assignments to Navy training and fighter squadrons, mostly in San Diego, I went to Washington, DC, and served on the staff that supports the Joint Chiefs of Staff in the Pentagon. The "dogfights" were all on paper and I had no instructors to supervise or protect me; this was the real world at the highest level. There were many, many lessons. I followed that tour with another desk job, serving on the staff of a Navy vice admiral (3 stars) in Japan, with the US Seventh Fleet.

My wife, Laura—I met her in 1982, and you'll meet her in *Topgun Days*, if you haven't already—shared the adventures and travels. In fact, it was her idea to request the assignment to Japan, an idea that we both agreed was a great one.

While in that assignment I received the good news that I had been selected to command an F-14 squadron. To say that this was an honor would be an understatement. I was thrilled, proud, and excited to return to flying, especially in command of a fighter squadron. I reported to the RAG for refresher training in 1996, and then reported to VF-211. It was a challenging and rewarding assignment, as the squadron prepared for potential combat operations over Iraq and deployed aboard the carrier USS *Nimitz*. We patrolled the no-fly zone over southern Iraq in 1997–1998, always ready for immediate reaction if we were attacked by aircraft or surface-to-air weapons—guns, missiles, or both. We also practiced complex strike operations, usually in conjunction with US Air Force aircraft and sometimes allied aircraft. The commitment and high performance of the men and women of VF-211, officers and enlisted, as they overcame many obstacles operating aging Tomcats, was inspiring to me as their skipper. I tried to live up to their expectations.

I took my last F-14 flight in 1998 and finished with 2,500 flight hours as an F-14 RIO in my logbook. And then, after a brief assignment aboard the carrier USS *George Washington*, I retired from the Navy. I became a defense contractor in the Washington, DC, area. But as I now write about my Navy flying experiences, that part of my life seems like only yesterday.

It's yesterday for the mighty Tomcat, too. The F-14 retired from US Navy service in 2006. For all fighters, retirement is a fact of life.

The Tomcat enjoyed a long career for a fighter, although these days fighters of all types are serving much longer than those of the 1940s and 1950s, when innovations came quickly. The F-14's duties were assumed by the F/A-18 Hornet and Super Hornet. They are known as strike-fighters for their dual roles of air-to-ground and air-to-air combat—often on the same mission. Most F/A-18s are single seat, with highly-trained pilots flying the demanding missions assigned to the aircraft, but one of the four strike-fighter squadrons assigned to each aircraft carrier includes a two-person crew. Instead of a RIO, the back-seater is now called a weapon system officer, or WSO—pronounced, of course, "whizzo."

The T-2, T-39, and TA-4 that I flew in Pensacola have also been retired, replaced by a new generation of trainer aircraft that include cutting-edge displays with better reliability. Even the simulators have been upgraded to match the aircraft and displays. All this powerful technology could barely be imagined when I went through Pensacola in 1979–80.

VT-10 and VT-86 remain on the job training SNFOs, joined now by a third squadron, VT-4, nicknamed Warbucks. In the "pipelines" chart in this book you'll notice a disparity in training for NFOs assigned to the E-2 and P-3 communities. VT-4 addresses that, providing crew training for them in Pensacola instead of at the other locations shown.

The pipelines chart also shows the number of aircraft available to NFOs in the Fleet, shown at right edge. In 1980 the Navy assigned NFOs to more than ten different models of aircraft. By 2015 this number has dropped to around eight, and is set to drop further as older types retire. Flying fewer aircraft types pays dividends. You need fewer supply chains, and maintenance training is streamlined, since each type requires unique training for the skilled technicians who repair and maintain it. Of course, the Navy must be sure that the aircraft can handle the different missions it has been assigned.

When the Cold War ended in 1991, US military forces began to shrink; that's known as the drawdown. The Navy operated fourteen aircraft carriers in 1980; it had ten at the beginning of 2015.* On the other hand, "smart weapons" such as GPS-guided bombs have increased the effectiveness of each bomb, and thus each aircraft that carries it. Such developments affect the number of students trained each year. When I graduated from VT-86, I was one of 451 student NFOs who won their wings in 1980. In 2014, there were 306—a reduction of one-third. (The Navy designated 1,084 new pilots in 2014. All numbers in this paragraph represent Navy and Marine Corps officers.)

New aircraft, new squadrons, fewer graduates. Staff job, overseas assignment, squadron command. Perspective. The most profound thought I can offer is that I had no idea where I would end up when I was sitting in that Pensacola classroom in July 1979.

Go ahead, ask me: Is there another book here? I'm glad you asked. Stay tuned.

Bio out.

* This includes only fixed-wing carriers, not the helicopter carriers used for amphibious operations.

# Glossary

*The definitions below refer to how these terms were used in this story, US Navy aviation operations around 1980.*

**15C9:** Simulator that included a realistic radar presentation and flight instruments. Now obsolete.

**1D23:** Basic aircrew task trainer. Did not represent an actual aircraft, but introduced students to navigation, communications, and other flight responsibilities.

**1v1:** One versus one.

**A-6 Intruder:** Sophisticated, two-seat air-to-ground attack jet used by US Navy (until 1997) and Marine Corps (until 1993). Built by Grumman. The letter A in the designation indicates its mission is attack, which is air-to-ground.

**A-7 Corsair II:** Versatile single-seat air-to-ground attack jet used by the US Navy until 1991. Built by Ling-Temco-Vought.

**ACM:** Air combat maneuvering, a training event where two or more aircraft perform high-performance turns, climbs, and dives in attempts to get into position to simulate firing missiles or guns at their opponent.

**Aerobatics:** Precision maneuvering in an aircraft.

**AFB:** Air force base.

**Afterburner or burner:** A device to increase the thrust of a jet engine. Consists of a tube that extends from the end of the engine, with pure fuel injected into it and ignited.

**AI:** Aviation Indoctrination, the first six weeks of training for all future Navy pilots and Naval Flight Officers. Has been renamed Aviation Preflight Indoctrination (API).

**Ailerons:** Movable surfaces on the wings of many aircraft that are used for maneuvering. The F-14 did not have ailerons.

**AIM-7 Sparrow:** Medium range air-to-air missile carried by many types of aircraft. Guided by radar, it is 12 feet long, weighs 500 pounds, and has a maximum range of roughly 30 miles. Being replaced by the newer AIM-120 AMRAAM.

**AIM-9 Sidewinder:** Short to medium range air-to-air missile carried by many types of aircraft. Seeks the infrared (heat) of the target, it is roughly 10 feet long and weighs less than 200 pounds, with a range up to 20 miles. Widely used, with updated versions still in service.

**AIM-54 Phoenix:** Long-range air-to-air missile, carried only by F-14s. Guided by radar, it was 13 feet long, weighed 1,000 pounds, and had a maximum range of 100 miles. No longer in use in the United States.

**Air Boss:** Unofficial name for the Air Department Officer on an aircraft carrier, he runs the 600-person Air Department and is responsible for operations on the flight deck and in the air around the carrier.

**Air-to-air:** Weapons and missions that attack other aircraft in flights.

**Air-to-ground:** Weapons and missions that attack targets on the ground.

**Airwing:** Collective term for the squadrons on an aircraft carrier. In the 1980s these typically included two fighter squadrons (air-to-air), three attack squadrons (air-to-ground), one electronic warfare squadron, one anti-submarine warfare squadron, one airborne early warning squadron, one helicopter squadron, and sometimes a small number of additional aircraft. There were variations to this structure. The total number of aircraft aboard was roughly eighty.

**Altitude chamber:** A training structure for exposing aircrews to the dangers of operating at high altitudes, which have lower air pressure and levels of oxygen.

**Angle of attack:** The angle at which an aircraft's wings meet the airstream. The term applies to all aircraft and is not related to weapons.

**AOCS:** Aviation Officer Candidate School, formerly a training program for college graduates who wanted to enter Naval Aviation and had not gone through ROTC. In 2007 AOCS was combined with the Navy's regular Officer Candidate School (OCS).

**AQM-37:** An unmanned target for air-to-air missiles.

**AQT/FAR:** Aviation Qualification Test / Flight Aptitude Record, tests formerly used as one of the qualifications to enter Navy flight training. Have been replaced by the Aviation Selection Test Battery (ASTB).

**Arresting cable:** The multi-strand steel cable on an aircraft carrier that is caught by the aircraft tailhook to bring aircraft to a stop. Diameter varies from one to almost one and a half inches. For decades US carriers had four arresting cables, but starting with the new carrier USS *George H. W. Bush* there are three. Also known as a cross deck pendant.

**Attack aircraft:** An aircraft with the primary mission of attacking ground targets. Designated by the letter A, such as A-4.

**Attitude:** An aircraft's orientation. For example, nose-high attitude refers to an aircraft flying with its nose above the horizon.

**AWG-9:** The F-14A Tomcat's radar and weapons control system (WCS).

**Bag:** Slang for a flight suit.

**Bagging traps:** Slang for making repeated landings on an aircraft carrier.

**Ball:** Short name for the optical landing system (OLS) that pilots use as a reference for carrier landings.

**Bearing:** The direction to an object or target in degrees, with reference to north on the compass or your own aircraft's nose.

**Bingo:** Condition when aircraft fuel reaches a level where the aircraft should stop performing its mission, whether training or combat, and return to base or head for aerial refueling.

**BN:** Bombardier/Navigator, the Naval Flight Officer in an A-6 Intruder.

**Bogey:** Any radar contact. In my early years of flying the term was often used imprecisely, and later we used *bogey* to indicate an unknown aircraft and *bandit* to indicate an enemy.

**Boldface:** Steps in emergency procedures that had to be memorized verbatim and performed in the event of a specific emergency. The F-14A pocket checklist (PCL) listed corrective actions for 93 specific emergencies. Of these, 23 emergencies with a total of 81 steps had to be committed to memory.

**Bomb:** A weapon used against a ground target. May be unpowered and unguided, but guided bombs ("smart bombs") have become more common. Some bombs have a small rocket motor to allow them to be dropped/launched at a distance from the target.

**BOQ:** Bachelor officers' quarters.

**Bouncing:** Slang term for field carrier landing practice (see *FCLP*).

**Bow:** The front of a ship.

**Break:** A maximum-performance turn that could be used to help tactical aircraft return to an airfield or carrier faster, as they would fly back at high speed and then perform a break turn overhead, slowing quickly to landing speed. Also used during the mission in response to a threatening aircraft or missile. Due to aerodynamics (induced drag associated with lift), a break turn caused the aircraft to rapidly lose speed.

**Brief/debrief:** The brief is a session where the upcoming flight is discussed. The debrief is held after the flight.

**Bulkhead:** Navy term for a wall on a ship.

**C-2 Greyhound:** Cargo aircraft that can land and takeoff from an aircraft carrier. Built by Northrop Grumman, still in service. The letter C in the designation indicates its mission is cargo.

**C-9 Skytrain:** Military cargo jet based on the DC-9 airliner. Built by McDonnell Douglas; recently retired by the Navy.

**Callsign:** An aviator's *nom de guerre*, used because aviators didn't want to use real names on the radio, and there could be multiple people with the same name. Callsigns basically replaced given names in squadrons.

**Canopy:** The clear covering above an aircraft cockpit, usually a strong plastic in modern tactical aircraft.

**Catapult, or cat:** The device that launches aircraft from carriers, capable of accelerating a 60,000 plus-pound fighter from zero to 150 mph in about two seconds (in concert with the fighter's engines). US carriers have four catapults. For decades, US carriers used steam catapults, but starting with USS *Gerald R. Ford* an electromagnetic catapult will be deployed. As this is written, *Ford* is scheduled to join the Fleet in 2016.

**Cat shot:** Launched from the catapult of an aircraft carrier.

**CH-46 Sea Knight:** A versatile twin-engine helicopter that was used by the US Navy and Marine Corps starting in 1964. Built by Boeing Vertol; retired from Navy service in 2004 and the Marine Corps in 2015.

**Checklist:** A standard list of procedures to be followed for various critical phases of a flight. The F-14A takeoff checklist had seventeen steps, and the landing checklist had ten.

**Chocks:** Objects that can be placed above and/or behind aircraft tires to keep them from rolling. Made of wood, hard rubber, plastic, or metal.

**Clearance Delivery:** The air traffic control agency that coordinates an aircraft flight plan with other agencies, allowing for safe and orderly start of a flight.

**Closing speed:** The combined speed of two aircraft approaching each other. If one aircraft is going 200 knots and another is flying toward it at 400 knots, their closing speed is 600 knots.

**CO:** Commanding officer, the senior officer of a squadron, can be either a pilot or NFO. In Navy squadrons, almost always called CO or Skipper by those in the squadron.

**Cockpit:** The area in an aircraft where the pilot sits, along with flight crew in multi-crew aircraft.

**Comm:** Communications.

**Control surfaces:** Collective term for the ailerons, elevators, rudders, and other movable devices on an aircraft that control its flight and cause it to maneuver.

**Control wipeout:** Moving the control stick to its limits, front and rear and side to side, to ensure the control surfaces move correctly and there are no restrictions to movement.

**CQ:** Carrier qualification, the rigorous process of training and certifying aviators for landing on aircraft carriers.

**Cross country:** Slang for a training flight to an airfield that is outside the normal operating area.

**Cruise:** Slang term for a deployment.

**Cut lights:** Lights on the carrier's optical landing system used to signal the approaching pilot without making a radio transmission.

**Debrief:** See *Brief*.

**Departure Control:** Air traffic control agency responsible for aircraft that leave the immediate area of the airfield (where the tower is responsible) and before they switch to the en route [?] air traffic control system.

**Deployment:** An extended period of real-world operations away from home station. Navy deployments in the 1970s and early 1980s were 7½ months, or longer during the Vietnam War. After the war, aircraft carriers demonstrated US national interests and exercised with friendly nations on deployment. In the mid-1980s, typical deployments were shortened to six months. This lasted until early in the twenty-first century when the demands of combat in several locations again increased deployment length.

**Detachment, or det:** When a unit or part of a unit leaves home station for a short period of time, typically one week to one month but may be longer. A det can refer to the entire operation away from home station, or can refer to the portion of the unit that performs the mission.

**Dilbert Dunker:** A training device that carries one person and plunges into a pool to familiarize aircrew with underwater egress. It is relatively basic, but an effective introduction to unfamiliar situations.

**Dogfight:** Slang term for aggressive close-in maneuvering by opposing aircraft. It can be two opponents (1v1) or many aircraft on either or both sides (many v many).

**Down:** A failing grade on a training event.

**Drag, thrust, gravity, and lift:** The four forces affecting an aircraft in flight. Thrust comes from the engine (jet, propeller, rocket). Drag is the opposite of thrust; it is the resistance of the air against an object pushing through it. Lift is generated by airflow over the wings and any other surfaces that are appropriately designed. Gravity, familiar to all humans, is the opposite of lift.

**E-2 Hawkeye:** An important command-and-control and airborne radar aircraft with a distinctive circular radar dome (radome) above the fuselage. Crew of five, consisting of two pilots in the cockpit and three NFOs in the fuselage. Built by Northrop Grumman.

**EA-6 Prowler:** Electronic warfare and attack jet based on the A-6 Intruder, with a crew of one pilot and three NFOs. Built by Northrop Grumman, remains in service with the US Marine Corps.

**Ejection seat:** A seat that can rapidly carry aircrews out of an aircraft in case of an emergency, usually rocket powered and equipped with a parachute. Has evolved into a very complex and capable system.

**Engagement:** General term for one aircraft attacking another. Similar to a dogfight.

**Enlisted personnel:** The largest component of a military force, who man the ranks performing warfare-specialized or technical tasks. Enlisted personnel may have college degrees, but a degree is generally not required.

**F-14 Tomcat:** A large, sophisticated, highly maneuverable aircraft that began service as an air-to-air fighter and evolved into a multi-mission strike-fighter. Retired from US Navy service in 2006. Built by Grumman, who had a tradition of naming fighter aircraft after cats.

**F-4 Phantom:** A versatile, sophisticated aircraft used by the US Navy, Marine Corps, and Air Force in many roles: strike-fighter, reconnaissance, and more. Retired from US Navy service in 1987; Marine Corps in 1992; Air Force in 1996. Built by McDonnell Douglas, and McDonnell had a tradition of giving occult names to fighters.

**FCLP:** Field carrier landing practice, which is training at an airfield to land on an aircraft carrier.

**Fighter aircraft:** An aircraft with the primary mission of attacking and destroying other aircraft.

**Fight's on:** The radio call to begin a training intercept or dogfight.

**Flaps:** The movable surfaces at the trailing edge of a wing that increase lift, primarily for takeoff and landing.

**Flight hours:** Normally the length of time from takeoff to landing, recorded in hours and tenths. Used for aircrew logbooks as well as scheduling aircraft maintenance.

**Flight line:** The area of an airfield between hangars and runways, where aircraft are parked. Also called the ramp.

**Flight side:** On a large base such as NAS Pensacola, the part of the base that consists of the runways, flight line, and hangars.

**Flight suit:** An aviator's coverall, usually made of flame-resistant Nomex fabric.

**Formation:** A well-defined group of two or more aircraft. Each type of aircraft has specific reference points that pilots use to remain in formation, and to make the formation consistent if there are more than two aircraft. In tactical formations the aircraft fly much farther apart.

**Foul deck:** Temporary condition of an aircraft carrier landing area when it is not ready for an aircraft to land. The most common cause is that an aircraft that just landed is still taxiing out of the landing area, but can also be caused by personnel or vehicles.

**FRS:** Fleet replacement squadron or fleet readiness squadron; it changed over the years. A squadron whose mission was to train aviators for a specific type of aircraft. See *RAG*.

**Fuselage:** The body of an aircraft.

**G:** The force of gravity, but usually refers to increased forces upon an aircraft and crew caused by a turn. A plane (or any vehicle) traveling straight and level at a constant speed experiences 1 g, Earth's gravity. Making a tight turn at high speed can increase the force to 6 g or more, making everything feel like it weighs six times as much: your head, your helmet, your arm.

**Gas and go:** Slang for a brief refueling stop, usually on a cross-country flight en route to the destination.

**Gear:** Can be a general term for equipment, or may refer to aircraft landing gear, depending on context.

**GPS:** The Global Positioning System, an extremely accurate means of determining an object's position using specialized equipment that processes signals from satellites.

***Gravity:*** *See Drag.*

**Ground Control:** The controlling agency that directs traffic on the flight line at an airfield, taxiing to or from the runway.

**G-suit:** An inflatable garment worn tight around the lower abdomen and legs that automatically inflates to squeeze the lower portion of the body when the aircraft is pulling g's. This reduces pooling of blood, keeping more of it in the upper body and supplying blood to the brain. It really works.

**Helo:** Slang term for a helicopter.

**Helo Dunker:** A training device carrying several people that descends into a pool, to provide training in underwater egress from a helicopter after a crash.

**Hop:** Slang term for a flight.

**Horizontal stabilizer:** The small wing-like objects that extend from the tail area of an aircraft.

**ICS:** Inter-cockpit communication system. The method of aircrew communicating with each other inside the aircraft.

**IFR:** Instrument flight rules. An extensive set of guidelines that govern flying operations. The alternative is VFR, visual flight rules, which allow more freedom.

**Inertial navigation:** A system that determines aircraft location based on precise measurements of gyroscopes within the aircraft.

**Intercept:** A series of maneuvers by a fighter that brings it into position to identify, escort, or destroy another aircraft.

**Kneeboard:** Rigid metal or plastic plate that is strapped to an aircrew's leg to hold cards and allow writing during the flight.

**Knock it off:** Standard radio call to end an engagement.

**Knot:** A measure of speed, nautical miles per hour. A nautical mile is 6,076 feet, which is about one sixth longer than a statute mile, so speed in knots is roughly 1⅙ times faster than the same number of miles per hour. Some common speeds converted to mph:
150 knots = 172 mph
300 knots = 345 mph
600 knots = 690 mph

**Landing gear:** The struts, wheels, tires, brakes, and associated parts that support the weight of an aircraft on the ground. Carrier-capable aircraft must have stout landing gear to withstand repeated carrier landings.

**Lead or flight lead:** The pilot who is in control of a group of aircraft. In a tactical situation, the lead can change quickly.

**Leave:** Military term for vacation.

**Lift:** See *Drag*.

**LSO:** Landing Signal Officer, a specially trained pilot who monitors carrier landings for safety and operating efficiency.

**Mach:** Ratio of aircraft speed to the speed of sound. Pronounced "mock." An aircraft going Mach 1 is flying at the speed of sound; at Mach 2 it is twice the speed of sound. The speed of sound varies based on temperature, altitude, and other conditions, but is approximately 660 knots or 760 mph at sea level.

**Mark or mark on top:** Verbal call made over ICS or radio to indicate the precise moment of an event, such flying overhead of a landmark.

**Max trap:** The maximum weight at which a carrier-capable aircraft can perform an arrested landing (trap). It is based on the aircraft's structure as well as the arresting gear's mechanical ability.

**Meatball:** See *Ball.*

**Merge plot:** The condition when two or more radar targets are very close to each other, when their radar blips have merged on the display. If a controller calls "merge plot" and the fighter does not have sight of the other aircraft, the fighter is likely in a defensive situation.

**Military power:** The maximum power level of an aircraft engine without engaging afterburner.

**Military ranks:** See table in next section.

**Missile:** General term for a flying object that has a guidance system and a power plant—usually a rocket engine. Missiles are made for air-to-air, air-to-ground, surface-to-air, and other applications.

**MISSILEX:** Missile exercise. Launching missile(s) at targets for training.

**NAMI:** The Naval Aerospace Medical Institute, NAS Pensacola, Florida.

**NAS:** Naval air station.

**NATOPS:** Naval Air Training and Operating Procedures.

**NFO:** Naval Flight Officer.

**Nomex:** A flame-resistant material used to make flight suits and other articles of clothing. A trademarked name. Flight suits are not flameproof or heatproof, but provide some protection in the event of a flash fire.

**Officers Club (or O-Club):** A structure on a military base for use by commissioned officers that includes a restaurant, bar, and often recreational facilities such as a swimming pool. Some

Navy bases and air stations also have enlisted clubs and chiefs clubs (for chief petty officers); others have all-ranks clubs.

**Optical Landing System:** See Ball.

**Outlying field:** A bare-bones airfield, usually with little more than a runway, simple control tower, and crash rescue crew. Often used for FCLPs.

**P-3 Orion:** Versatile anti-submarine and maritime surveillance aircraft; the P indicates patrol. Carries a crew of 11 or 12 and a large variety of sensors and weapons. Land-based, not aircraft carrier-capable. Built by Lockheed.

**Paraloft:** Short for parachute loft, the place where parachutes were worked on in the early days of flying. Now often refers to a locker room for aircraft flight gear (helmets, parachute harnesses, g-suits, etc.).

**PCL:** Pocket checklist.

**Pickle:** A switch held by an LSO on a carrier flight deck that controls lights to signal approaching aircraft.

**Plane captain:** Usually an enlisted person who is responsible for an aircraft. In the US Navy, PCs are usually fairly new to a squadron, but they have broad responsibilities for routine inspection and servicing of aircraft, and preparing them for flight.

**POW:** Prisoner of war.

**Preflight/postflight:** Preflight is an orderly inspection of an aircraft to ensure that important systems are ready for flight. The official preflight inspection of an F-14A Tomcat with no weapons had 111 items. Postflight is a walk-around inspection after completion of a flight.

**PSI:** Pounds per square inch (pressure).

**Qual:** Short for qualification or qualified, depending on context.

**Radar lock:** The condition of a radar system when it is automatically tracking a target. Usually involves the antenna pointing at the target, and adjusting itself to continue pointing. This results in the most accurate information, but the radar cannot see other targets when it is locked. The F-14's

AWG-9 and modern radars can provide accurate information about multiple targets without being locked on to only one.

**RAG:** Replacement air group. Term for a squadron dedicated to training aviators for a specific type of aircraft. The official name was changed to fleet readiness squadron, but the term RAG continued in common usage.

**Ready room:** The room on an aircraft carrier or in a hangar on an air base from which a squadron manages its operations. The SDO sits in the ready room. The hub of a squadron.

**RIO:** Radar intercept officer.

**Rocket:** General term for a powered but unguided flying object. Can be used for air-to-ground, and in some forms for air-to-air. Compare to *missile*.

**Roger:** Radio or ICS reply indicating that a statement is received and understood. Does not necessarily mean that you will follow an instruction; that is "wilco," for *will comply*.

**ROTC:** Reserve Officer Training Corps.

**RTB:** Return to base.

**Rudder:** The movable surface at the rear of the vertical tail of an aircraft which controls movement of the nose left and right.

**Runway:** The long, level surface at an airfield used for takeoffs and landings. Usually made of concrete.

**S-3 Viking:** Carrier-based anti-submarine and maritime surveillance aircraft, with a crew of four. Built by Lockheed. Retired from Fleet service in 2009.

**SA:** Situational awareness.

**SDO:** Squadron duty officer.

**SERE:** Survival, evasion, resistance, and escape; a training course.

**Shooter:** Officer who stands near the catapult on an aircraft carrier, verifies all checks have been completed, and all personnel and equipment are ready for launch. The Shooter accepts the final salute from the pilot and then dramatically sweeps his/her arm forward and touches the flight deck, signaling for the Launch button to be pushed, and the aircraft is going flying.

**Simulator, or sim:** A ground-based training device that may be a simple cockpit or a complete, accurate replication of an aircraft.

**Skipper:** Common term for the commanding officer of a squadron. Though it may sound casual, it is a term of respect.

**SNA:** Student Naval Aviator, a student pilot in the Navy.

**SNFO:** Student Naval Flight Officer, who is preparing to be aircrew, but not a pilot.

**Soviet Union:** A political entity, a federation of fifteen republics that spanned Europe and Asia. Dissolved in 1991.

**Speed brakes:** Movable panels that are normally recessed, but can be extended to increase drag and thus slow an aircraft.

**Spotlighting:** Manually adjusting a radar antenna in elevation to match the elevation of a target. Compare to radar lock.

**Squadron:** An organization that operates aircraft. In the Navy, a squadron included maintenance and administrative personnel, in addition to aircrews. Squadron size varied by type: in the 1980s, F-14 squadrons had twelve aircraft, S-3 squadrons had 10 aircraft, and E-2 squadrons had four to six aircraft. In my experience we never called it a squad.

**Stall:** Condition that occurs when a wing increases its angle too much, the air no longer flows smoothly over it, and the wing loses lift. Can be dangerous if it occurs near the ground or if the pilot does not apply the proper controls in response to the stall.

**State:** The amount of fuel aboard an aircraft, often given in thousands and hundreds of pounds. For example, "state eight point six" indicates 8,600 pounds of fuel. Can also be reported as "state tiger," which indicates enough fuel and weapons to perform a mission.

**Strike fighter:** An aircraft that performs air-to-air and air-to-ground missions well. In addition to the obvious, aircraft and weapon system design, aircrew training and weapons load are important considerations.

**Subsonic/supersonic:** Subsonic aircraft cannot safely exceed Mach 1, the speed of sound (see Mach). Supersonic aircraft are designed to operate at speeds above Mach 1.

**T-2 Buckeye:** A jet-powered basic trainer used by the US Navy for pilot and NFO training. Built by North American Aviation. Retired in 2008.

**T-39 Sabreliner:** Converted from a business jet, used for training NFOs. Built by North American Aviation. Retired in 2014.

**TA-4 Skyhawk:** Variant of the small, maneuverable A-4 attack jet, the TA-4 was used to train pilots and NFOs. Built by McDonnell Douglas. Retired from Navy service in 2003, from Marine Corps service in 1998.

**TACAN:** Tactical air navigation system.

**TACTS:** Tactical Aircrew Combat Training System. Also known as ACMI—Air Combat Maneuvering Instrumentation. A system of ground receiving stations, transmitters in aircraft, processors and displays that provides an accurate, high-quality depiction of aircraft. Useful for real-time observation but especially for debriefs.

**Tail:** The rear of an airplane. An imprecise term that may refer to the vertical stabilizers or horizontal stabilizers.

**Tailhook:** Strong hook at the end of a steel tube, which catches the arresting cable on aircraft carriers. The assembly on an F-14 is more than seven feet long. Most military aircraft have arresting hooks for emergency use, but those on Navy carrier-based aircraft were designed for the stress of repeated arrested landings.

**Tally-ho:** Radio transmission indicating the aircrew has sight of an enemy aircraft.

**Target drone:** An unmanned flying vehicle used for missile exercises. Some are only slightly larger than the air-to-air missiles that intercept them, while others are conversions of full-size aircraft originally flown by aircrews.

**Throttle:** The lever in a cockpit that controls engine speed. Mounted on the left instrument panel in most tactical aircraft.

**Thrust:** See *Drag*.

**TID:** Tactical information display, in an F-14.

**Topgun:** Unofficial name for the Navy Fighter Weapons School, which was established in 1969 to provide "post-graduate" training for combat aircrews.

**Touch and go:** A brief landing, at an airfield or aircraft carrier, when the aircraft does not intend to stop. Instead of applying the brakes or using the tailhook, the pilot adds power at touchdown and flies away again.

**Tour:** Time served at a specific squadron, ship, or other assignment. In the Navy, many tours are three years, although they can vary greatly.

**Tower:** The air traffic control facility that controls flying traffic in the vicinity of an airfield.

**Trap:** Slang term for an arrested landing.

**Vertical stabilizer:** The fin that extends from the top of the rear fuselage and provides yaw stability (left-and-right) on an aircraft in flight.

**VFR:** Visual flight rules. See *IFR*.

**Wave-off:** Command for a pilot to abort an approach, add power and climb, when an intended landing should not be made. A wave-off usually indicates an unexpected situation, such as an aircraft or vehicle that was expected to be clear is still in the landing area or on the runway.

**Waypoint:** A specific location along a route, usually expressed in latitude and longitude but may be described as a visually significant object.

**Wilco:** Will comply. See *Roger*.

**Windscreen:** The fixed forward part of the canopy.

**Wingman:** The second aircraft in a two-plane formation. Often supports the first aircraft, which is the lead.

**XO:** Executive officer, the second in command of a Navy squadron. Can be either a pilot or NFO. In Navy squadrons, moves up to the CO job when the current CO completes his tour or if he is lost.

APPENDIX

# US Navy Ranks and Rates

Uniformed personnel in the US military fall into three categories that can be briefly summarized as follows:

Officers can hold positions of greater responsibility, and are normally "commissioned" after completing a service academy, ROTC in college, or officer candidate program. A college degree is required for officers.

Enlisted personnel are those who man the ranks, performing warfare-specialized or technical tasks. Enlisted personnel may have college degrees, but a degree is generally not required.

In between are a limited number of warrant officers, who are so designated based on technical expertise.

Officer Ranks (most junior at the top of the list)

| Navy Rank | Pay Grade | Abbreviation | Collar Insignia | Other Services Equivalent |
|---|---|---|---|---|
| Ensign | O-1 | ENS | One gold bar | Second Lieutenant |
| Lieutenant (junior grade) | O-2 | LTJG | One silver bar | First Lieutenant |
| Lieutenant | O-3 | LT | Two silver bars | Captain |
| Lieutenant Commander | O-4 | LCDR | Gold oak leaf | Major |
| Commander | O-5 | CDR | Silver oak leaf | Lieutenant Colonel |
| Captain | O-6 | CAPT | Eagle | Colonel |
| Rear Admiral (lower half) | O-7 | RDML | One star | Brigadier General |
| Rear Admiral | O-8 | RADM | Two stars | Major General |
| Vice Admiral | O-9 | VADM | Three stars | Lieutenant General |
| Admiral | O-10 | ADM | Four stars | General |

**Enlisted Rates (most junior at the top of the list)**

| Navy Rate | Pay Grade | Collar Insignia | Army Equivalent |
|---|---|---|---|
| Airman Recruit | E-1 | None | Private |
| Airman Apprentice | E-2 | None | Private |
| Airman | E-3 | None | Private First Class |
| Petty Officer Third Class | E-4 | Eagle and one chevron | Specialist or Corporal |
| Petty Officer Second Class | E-5 | Eagle and two chevrons | Sergeant |
| Petty Officer First Class | E-6 | Eagle and three chevrons | Staff Sergeant |
| Chief Petty Officer | E-7 | Fouled anchor | Sergeant First Class |
| Senior Chief Petty Officer | E-8 | Fouled anchor with star | Master Sergeant or First Sergeant |
| Master Chief Petty Officer | E-9 | Fouled anchor with two stars | Command Sergeant Major |

Notes about enlisted rates:

The names given for E-1 through E-3 are for personnel in aviation fields. Personnel may also be known as Seaman, Fireman, or Constructionman.

More senior to E-9 are the special ranks Command Master Chief, Fleet/Force Master Chief, and Master Chief Petty Officer of the Navy.

The Air Force and Marine Corps have different names for enlisted ranks.

# Acknowledgments

I would like to thank the following people for their assistance and support with this project:

My wife, Laura, has once again proven to be an excellent editor, proofreader, and advisor.

Former F-14 pilot, squadronmate, and Topgun instructor Paul "Nick" Nickell generously contributed several well-written paragraphs that give the pilot and LSO perspectives of a carrier landing.

Aviation photographers David F. Brown, Dave "HeyJoe" Parsons (a former F-14 RIO), and Cédric Bernard responded quickly to my requests for assistance by providing key photos.

Skyhorse Publishers continues to be a pleasure to work with.

Writing this book has been an enjoyable experience overall, and one of the unexpected bright spots has been working with my editor, David "TOD" Robinson (who happened to have been a Navy pilot). Our chance meeting proved fortuitous, and I've enjoyed his editorial guidance as well as his friendship.

# Index